P9-DMZ-098

# Across the Plains
# in the Donner Party

# Across the Plains in

*Edited by Karen Zeinert*

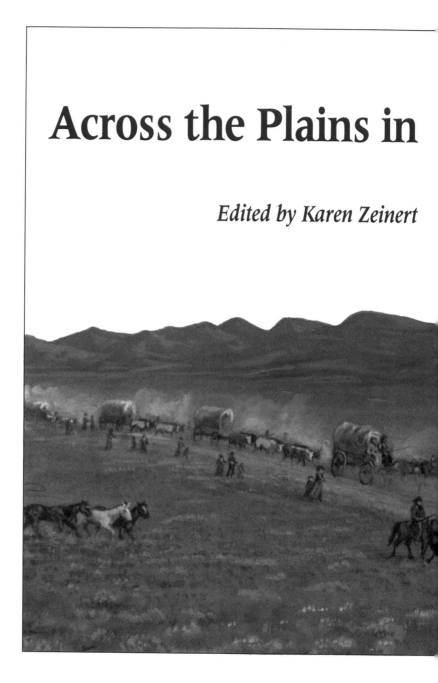

LIBRARY MEDIA CENTER
MIDDLETOWN HIGH SCHOOL
Hunting Hill Ave.
Middletown, CT

# the Donner Party

*by Virginia Reed Murphy*
*with Letters by James Reed*

### Linnet Books   1996

© 1996 by Karen Zeinert. All rights reserved.
First published 1996 as a Linnet Book,
an imprint of The Shoe String Press, Inc.,
North Haven, Connecticut 06473.

Library of Congress Cataloging-in-Publication Data
Murphy, Virginia Reed, b. 1834?
Across the plains in the Donner Party / by Virginia Reed Murphy ;
with letters by James Reed ; edited by Karen Zeinert.
p.   cm.
Includes bibliographical references (p.   ).
ISBN 0-208-02404-2 (alk. paper)
1. Donner Party.   2. Murphy, Virginia Reed, b. 1834?—Journeys—
West (U.S.)   I. Reed, James Frazier, 1800–1874.   II. Zeinert,
Karen.   III. Title.
F868.N5M8   1996
979.4'03'092—dc20        95-52360
CIP

Baker & Taylor   1/99   17.50/16.3Y

The paper used in this publication meets the minimum
requirements of American National Standard for Information
Sciences—Permanence of Paper for Printed Library Materials,
ANSI Z39.48-1984. ♾

Designed by Abigail Johnston
Title page illustration: Platte River Valley by William Henry Jackson. Courtesy
of Scotts Bluff National Monument.

Printed in the United States of America

*To my mother, Burdella O'Niel,*
*who planned our family's first journey*
*across the plains to California*

# Contents

# Contents

# Introduction

When the members of the Donner wagon train left Illinois in 1846 to start a long, dangerous trek to California, which was then owned by Mexico, they did so because of the promising stories that they had read about the territory. For years, writers who had visited California had been describing its great beauty, its gentle ocean breezes, and its generous land grants.

One of the most popular writers of the day, Richard Henry Dana, said that California was a paradise. He claimed that this exotic land had the most perfect climate in the whole world as well as an abundance of resources, "good harbors, forests in the north, waters filled with fish, plains covered with thousands of herds of cattle, and soil in which corn yield[ed] from seventy to eighty-fold." Dana's readers, especially farmers in the Midwest, were awestruck by such descriptions.

Another writer, former American John Marsh, who moved to California in 1836, also wrote about California's wonders. He led an impressive letter-to-the-editor campaign in newspapers throughout the United States to try to convince Americans to join him. Although most writers simply wanted to share their impressions of California with their readers, Marsh had a different purpose in mind: He owned huge tracts of land that he wanted to sell. He knew that hundreds—maybe even thousands!—of settlers rushing to California would drive up land prices and make a tidy profit for him.

Besides describing all that California had to offer, Marsh bragged that people could do as they pleased in his area without any trouble from the Mexican government. While this was of great importance to Marsh, who practiced medicine without a license, few emigrants rushed westward to join him. In fact, only two hundred Americans had moved to California by 1842.

The small number of Americans in the area was the result of two deeply held concerns. First, few wanted to live under Mexican rule, even if Marsh said that citizens could do as they wished. Second, no direct overland trail to California had been found through the massive Sierra Nevada Mountains, which run most of the length of California's eastern border. To avoid the mountains, travelers had to journey south of the Sierras, through a desert where daytime temperatures could soar to 120° F., or they had to journey north of the mountains, going to the Oregon Territory before swinging south to their destination. Both trips were grueling, dangerous ordeals.

Because the overland trek was so difficult, many emigrants who wanted to go to California went there by sea. Travelers had to board a ship on the East Coast, sail all the way around the tip of South America, then head north for over six thousand miles up the western coast to reach California. This journey was anything but short or fast or cheap. Those who wished to cut their sea voyage in half could sail south as far as the Isthmus of Panama in Central America, a narrow neck of land about fifty miles wide, where the Panama Canal would later be built in 1904. They crossed it on foot and then sailed north to California on another ship. Hiking across the isthmus was difficult and risky because this area was hot, swampy, and full of mosquitoes, some of which carried yellow fever and malaria.

So explorers and would-be guides, encouraged by men like Marsh, continued to search for passes through the mountains. By 1841, they had found several routes through the Sierras. However, these passes weren't wide enough to accommodate wagons. It took three more years of searching before an adequate opening was located. This site eventually would become known as the Donner Pass.

The first party to use the newly found route was led by Elisha Stevens in 1844. The trail was extremely difficult, and some mountain ridges were so steep that the oxen pulling the wagons could not keep their footing. In order to cross, the California-bound settlers had to take some time-consuming, backbreaking steps. First, they unloaded every item from their prairie schooners, removed the wagons' canvas tops to reduce the weight, and lifted the wagons over the ridges with the help of pulleys and ropes. The settlers then carried all of their belongings over the ridges to their wagons and repacked them. Although the Stevens train proved that it was possible to cross the Sierras with wagons, the hardships it endured did not encourage many people to follow.

Even so, promoters continued to praise the area's climate and resources. One of the best known of these promoters was twenty-three-year-old Lansford W. Hastings, who had traveled extensively in California. In 1844, he went back East to the United States to speak about California and promote his book, *The Emigrant's Guide to Oregon and California,* a text that made the journey to California sound a lot easier than it was. Hastings traveled throughout the Ohio Valley—which includes parts of Illinois, Indiana, Ohio, Kentucky, Pennsylvania, New York, and West Virginia—during 1844. He offered his services as a guide to would-be emigrants, hoping to entice as many as possible to the Pacific Ocean. Hastings was a man of big dreams. He planned to seize California from Mexico with the help of fellow Americans and then install himself as its leader.

Lansford Hastings was a persuasive talker, too, and as a result, interest in moving to California was very high by 1845. This was especially true in the Midwest where winters were, and still are, very long and very cold. California's mild climate had special appeal there. Also, an economic depression had caused financial hardships—even ruin—for many Midwestern farmers and businessmen, and a chance to start over was tempting. In addition, a war between the United States and Mexico appeared certain. Americans expected, correctly, to win such a war, after which the United States could exercise its "manifest destiny" and lay claim to several Mexican holdings it had been eyeing, including California. This meant that emigrants could hope to be part of the United States again, and the fear of living under Mexican rule was greatly diminished.

*Lansford W. Hastings wrote* The Emigrant's Guide to Oregon and California *which made the overland trek to the Pacific Coast sound easy. It was the shortcut he suggested that put the Donner party on the trail to disaster. Courtesy of the Utah State Historical Society.*

In Springfield, Illinois, three families were so impressed with Hastings's book that they made plans to go to California in the spring of 1846. These families were headed by George Donner, his brother Jacob Donner, and James Reed.

George and Jacob Donner were both in their sixties.

Born of German parents in North Carolina, they had moved west by stages, settling first in Kentucky, then Indiana, and finally, Illinois. Although they were prosperous farmers, the depression in the Midwest had caused economic setbacks for both.

George had been married three times. Both his first and second wives had died at an early age. His third wife, Tamsen, who had lost her husband and two young daughters in a cholera epidemic, was a teacher. She wanted to start an academy for girls in California, and she spent most of the winter of 1845–46 packing materials, especially books, for her future students. George and Tamsen had three children, and Mr. Donner had two daughters from his second marriage who still lived with him. The children from his first marriage were adults by 1846 and living on their own.

The head of the other Donner family, Jacob, was in poor health, and he looked forward to living in a warmer climate. His wife, Elizabeth, who had been a widow before she married Jacob, had two children from her first marriage. The Donners had five children of their own.

James Reed had been born in Ireland. His father's ancestors had been Polish nobles who had left their homeland rather than bow down to leaders they considered poor rulers. His mother was of Scotch-Irish ancestry. Reed's parents had moved to America when he was very young, and he had spent most of his life in Illinois. In 1846, Reed was forty-six years old and a wealthy cabinetmaker who also was facing economic problems due to the recession. He was strong and able and very self-confident.

*Virginia's parents, James and Margaret Reed, are pictured here. Unfortunately there are no known photographs of Virginia Reed as a child. Courtesy of the California Department of Parks and Recreation.*

Reed had married Margaret Keyes Backenstoe, a widow with a young daughter named Virginia, whom he adopted. Mrs. Reed, like Jacob Donner, was also suffering from poor health, and she, too, looked forward to a better climate in California. The Reeds had three children of their own.

All three families hired help, such as drivers and choregirls, for the long and difficult trip. This was a common practice among wealthy families, for it greatly reduced the amount of their work. This practice also enabled poor men and women who were willing to work their way to California to make the trip at little or no cost. Once in California, they hoped to receive a generous land grant and start a new, prosperous life.

The Donners and the Reeds, with their nine wagons, formed a small wagon train. As the train headed west, it was joined by other families at various points along the way and eventually grew to include forty wagons. When George Donner was chosen to be the leader, the group became known as the Donner party.

Unlike many other wagon trains, the Donner party did not have a guide, nor did anyone in the group have any idea of the difficulties that awaited them. None of them had ever undertaken a two-thousand-mile overland trip before, nor had they ever seen a desert that took days to cross or mountains the size of the Sierras, which are over 8,000 feet tall. None of them had experienced a mountain blizzard, either, which, unlike Midwestern snowstorms, could last for a week at a time, depositing unbelievable amounts of snow each day and stranding travelers until spring. Confident that they could handle any problems that came their way, the party, with its heavily loaded wagons, chose to proceed at a leisurely pace instead of pushing across the plains as rapidly as possible. This choice proved to be disastrous.

The Donner party's journey to California is one of the most interesting and intriguing stories in American history. It is a life-and-death struggle full of heroes and villains that is still surrounded by questions and controversy even though it occurred 150 years ago and has been studied closely by many historians. Was the Donner party foolhardy—or incredibly brave—to undertake such a trip? Was the party's confidence a handicap or an asset? What role did fate play in the grim drama? And the most fascinating question of all—what really happened on that long journey to California?

# Part One

*Overleaf: Independence Rock by William Henry Jackson. Such land-marks guided the emigrants, who used them to measure mileage and estimate how far they had come. Courtesy of Scotts Bluff National Monument.*

# Editor's Note

The story of the Donner party's disastrous journey was first recorded in diaries and letters written along the way. After the trip was completed and rumors about the party's horrible experiences began to circulate, including shocking stories about cannibalism, newspaper reporters interviewed the survivors. These published articles grabbed the public's interest, and there was a demand for more information for many years to come.

In 1891, James Reed's stepdaughter, Virginia, who was by then Mrs. J. M. Murphy, was asked by Century magazine to write an article about her experiences in the Donner party. Her story, "Across the Plains in the Donner Party," is the most complete record written by a member of the party, and it is the foundation for the text that follows.

Virginia's words in Part One are supplemented by letters Mr. Reed wrote to relatives in the United States as he traveled west. He sent these letters home with men he met on the trail who were returning east. News about people heading to California was in such demand in the travelers' hometowns that their letters were given to local newspapers for publication. Reed's letters appeared in several issues of the Sangamo Journal in Springfield, Illinois, in 1846. To distinguish Reed's accounts from Virginia's story in the following pages, his letters have been put into separate chapters beneath his byline.

*A chronology, illustrations, charts, and maps have been added to make the story easier to understand. In addition, spelling and punctuation have been standardized for the reader's ease.*

*And finally, even though the names, dates, and events that Virginia described have been verified against numerous historical records, readers should remember that "Across the Plains in the Donner Party" is Virginia's version of what happened, written forty-five years after it took place. Not every survivor would have described these events exactly the way she did. The death of John Snyder, for instance, was seen as murder by some, but self-defense by Virginia. Even so, her story is an important contribution toward our understanding of what actually happened to the Donner party.*

*K. Z.*

# Chronology

| | |
|---|---|
| April 14, 1846 | The Donner party leaves Springfield, Illinois. The group includes 16 adults, 16 children, many horses, cattle, dogs, and 9 covered wagons drawn by oxen. The party carries enough food for a six-month trip. |
| May 29 | The wagon train, which is joined by others as it moves westward, stops at the swollen Big Blue River in northeast present-day Kansas, unable to cross. While the party waits for the river to go down, Virginia's Grandma Keyes dies and is buried in the wilderness on the site of what is now Manhattan, Kansas. The party crosses the river by building rafts for the wagons. |
| June 15 | James Reed and others hunt buffalo. |
| June 17 | The Donner party crosses the South Fork of the Platte River in what is now western Nebraska. |
| July 4 | The caravan arrives at Fort Laramie in what is now Wyoming and celebrates the Fourth with a toast to friends back in Springfield. |

| | |
|---|---|
| July 6 | The wagon train leaves Fort Laramie for Fort Bridger on the Green River in southwestern Wyoming, arriving there in late July. |
| July 31 | The Donner party leaves Fort Bridger, where members learned about a new route called the Hastings Cutoff that supposedly could shorten the trip by 300 to 400 miles. After much discussion, Reed and 73 others decide to take this route, while the rest of the party continues on the traditional trail. |
| August 6 | The Donner party arrives at Weber Canyon and finds a note from Lansford Hastings, who discovered the new route and is guiding a train ahead of them. Hastings tells the Donner party to abandon the cutoff and take another route to the Great Salt Lake through the Wasatch Mountains. The Graves group, a party of 13, joins the caravan, bringing its number to 87. |
| August 6–11 | The wagon train remains in camp while James Reed, C. T. Stanton, and William Pike search for Hastings for advice. |
| August 12–27 | The Donner party struggles over the Wasatch Mountains. |
| End of August | The train reaches the Great Salt Lake and prepares to cross the desert, resting first at a valley called Twenty Wells. |
| September 3–8 | The train crosses the Great Salt Lake desert. The cattle and oxen stampede when they finally smell water. |

September 9–15      The party holds an unsuccessful search for the animals before moving on. The Reeds have one cow and one ox and must abandon two of their three wagons and borrow oxen from others to pull their remaining wagon. Before leaving camp, the party takes an inventory of food. Because the train is very short of food, Charles Stanton and William McCutchen volunteer to go to Sutter's Fort, near Sacramento, and bring back supplies.

September 30      The Donner party reaches the old Fort Hall trail.

October 5      James Reed kills John Snyder in an argument near the Humboldt River on the old Fort Hall trail. Reed is banished from the wagon train, and he heads for Sutter's Fort.

October 13–14      The wagon train crosses a second desert between Humboldt Sink and Truckee River, where the fine sand makes travel extremely difficult.

Mid-October      James Reed meets Charles Stanton, who is returning to the train from Sutter's Fort with provisions. The men agree that the supplies will not be adequate, so Reed decides to continue on to Sutter's Fort to get more food. Meanwhile, Stanton is to deliver the food he has and lead the party over the summit of the Sierra Nevada mountains to the Bear River valley, where Reed will be waiting with additional supplies.

October 19          Stanton and two Indians from Sutter's
                    Fort reach the Donner party near Lake
                    Tahoe in what is now Nevada.

Late October        Reed reaches Sutter's Fort, where he
                    finds McCutchen recovering from his trip
                    to the fort with Stanton. They set out for
                    the Bear River valley with supplies. When
                    they arrive, the train is not in the valley,
                    so the men begin to work their way east
                    to find it. When the men are forced by
                    snow to turn back, they go to Johnson's,
                    then Sutter's Fort, for help.

October 31          The Donner party makes its first attempt
                    to cross the summit and fails, camping
                    within three miles of the summit. A
                    snowstorm arrives. The party is snow-
                    bound in the Sierras.

# The Drivers
# Cracked Their Whips
# and the
# Long Journey Began

*Virginia Reed Murphy*

Although I was only twelve years old when my family began its journey to California, I remember the trip well. I have every reason to do so, since the dangers and ordeals we faced were so extraordinary.

Our little band, which drove out of Springfield, Illinois, on April 14, 1846, has often been referred to as the "ill-fated Donner party." My father, James F. Reed, was the originator of the party, and the Donner brothers, George and Jacob, who lived just outside Springfield, decided to join him. All the previous winter, we prepared for the coming journey.

One of my main concerns was encountering Indians, the very thought of which frightened me no end. But right here let me say that we suffered vastly more from fear of the Indians before starting than we did on the plains; at least this was my case.

My fear was based on tales that I had heard and loved to have repeated. Grandma Keyes, who lived with us, used to tell me these stories. She had an aunt who had been taken prisoner by the Indians in an early settlement in Virginia and had remained a captive in their hands for five years before she made her escape. Evening after evening, I would go into Grandma's room and sit with my back close against the wall so that no warrior could slip behind me with a tomahawk. I would coax Grandma to tell me more about her aunt, and I would listen to the recital of the fearful deeds of the Indians until it seemed to me that everything in the room, from the high old-fashioned bedposts down to the shovel and tongs in the chimney corner, had been transformed into Indians in paint and feathers, all ready for the war dance. When I was told that we were going to California and would have to pass through a region peopled by Indians, you can imagine how I felt.

My mother, though a young woman, was not strong, and she had been in delicate health for many years. Yet when dangers came upon her on our way to California, she was the bravest of the brave. Grandma Keyes, who was seventy-five years old, was an invalid, confined to her bed. So the car in which both were to ride was planned to give comfort. Our wagons were all made to order, and I can say without fear of contradiction that nothing like our family wagon ever started across the plains. It was a two-story wagon that some called a "pioneer palace car." The entrance was on the side, like that of an old-fashioned stagecoach, and one stepped up and into a small room in

# The Donner Party
*Left Springfield, Illinois, April 14, 1846*
*(ages of members given in parentheses)*

*The Donner group—six wagons:*
George (62) and Tamsen (45) Donner
Their children: Frances (6), Georgia (4), and Eliza (3)
George's daughters from a previous marriage:
Elitha (14) and Leanna (12)

Jacob (65) and Elizabeth (45) Donner
Their children: George (9), Mary (7), Isaac (5),
Samuel (4), and Lewis (3)
Elizabeth's sons from a previous marriage:
Solomon (14) and William (12) Hook
A friend: John Denton (28)
Three drivers: Samuel Shoemaker (25),
Noah James (20?), and Hiram Miller (45?)

*The Reed group—three wagons*
James (46) and Margaret (32) Reed
Their children: Patty (8), James, Jr. (5),
and Thomas (3)
Margaret's daughter from a previous marriage:
Virginia (12)
Margaret's mother: Sarah Keyes (75?)
Three drivers: James Smith (25), Walter Herron (25),
and Milt Elliott (28)
A hired girl: Eliza Williams (25)
A handyman: Baylis Williams (24), Eliza's brother

the center of the wagon. At the right and left were spring seats with comfortable high backs, where we could sit and ride with as much ease as on the seats of a Concord coach. Under the spring seats were compartments in which were stored many articles useful for the journey. In this little room was a tiny stove for warmth, and its pipe, running through the top of the wagon, was circled with tin to keep it from setting fire to the canvas cover.

Boards running the full length of the wagon were fastened to a frame that spanned the width of the palace car, a frame that was located just above the wheels. These boards formed the foundation for a large, roomy second story that housed our beds. Our clothing was packed in strong canvas bags.

Some of Mama's young friends gave her a mirror in order, as they said, that my mother might not forget to keep her good looks. It hung directly opposite the door in the center room. Strangely enough, although we went over very rough terrain before we had to leave this wagon standing like a monument on the Salt Lake Desert, the glass never broke. I have often thought how pleased the Indians must have been when they found this mirror, which gave them back the picture of their own faces.

We also had two wagons loaded with provisions. Everything in that line that could be thought of was bought. My father started with supplies enough to last us through the first winter in California, if we made the journey in the usual time of six months. Knowing that books were always scarce in a new country, we also took a good library of standard works. We even took along a new cooking

*Prairie schooners were packed with everything a family would need for the long journey westward. Because the wagons were so crowded, most families also carried small tents to serve as sleeping quarters when they set up camp each night. Courtesy of the National Archives.*

stove. Certainly no family ever started across the plains with more provisions or a better outfit for the journey.

We had many animals with us: five dogs, saddle horses, cows, and oxen. The family wagon was drawn by four yoke of oxen, large Durham steers, and the two supply wagons were drawn on three yoke each. The other animals were led or herded along as we made our way to California.

I also had a pony. His name was Billy, and he was a beauty. I can scarcely remember when I was taught to sit a horse. I only know that when I was seven, I was the proud owner of a pony and that I used to go riding with Papa. The chief pleasure I looked forward to when crossing the plains was to ride my pony every day. But a day came when I had no pony to ride. The poor little fellow gave out, for he could not endure the hardships of ceaseless travel. When I was forced to part with him, I cried until I was ill, and I sat in the back of the wagon watching him become smaller and smaller as we drove on, until I could see him no more.

Never can I forget the morning when we bade farewell to kindred and friends. The Donners were there, having driven to our place the evening before so that we might get an early start. Grandma Keyes was carried out of the house and placed in the wagon on a large feather bed, propped up with pillows. Her sons in Springfield, Gersham and James W. Keyes, tried to dissuade her from the long and fatiguing journey, but in vain; she would not be parted from my mother, who was her only daughter. We were surrounded by loved ones, and there stood all my little schoolmates who had come to kiss me good-by. My father, with tears in his eyes, tried to smile as one friend after another grasped his hand in a last farewell. Mama was overcome with grief. When the last "good-by" was said, we climbed into the wagons. The drivers cracked their whips, and when the oxen moved forward, the long journey began.

I can still see our little caravan as we drove out of old Springfield. My little black-eyed sister Patty sat upon the

*Wagon trains heading west stopped on the edge of the frontier, in such cities as Independence and St. Louis, Missouri. Here pioneers replaced vital foodstuffs used up on the first part of the journey. There would be no further opportunity to purchase supplies until the travelers reached the first fort on the Oregon Trail, and even then, supplies would be limited. Courtesy of the Dover Pictorial Archives.*

bed in the family wagon, holding up the wagon cover so that Grandma might have a last look at her old home.

In addition to the wagon train, many friends joined us for a few miles, and some camped with us the first night out. My uncles traveled on for several days before bidding us a final farewell.

Milt [Elliott], a knight of the whip, drove our family wagon. He had worked in my father's large sawmill on the Sangamon River for many years. It seemed strange to

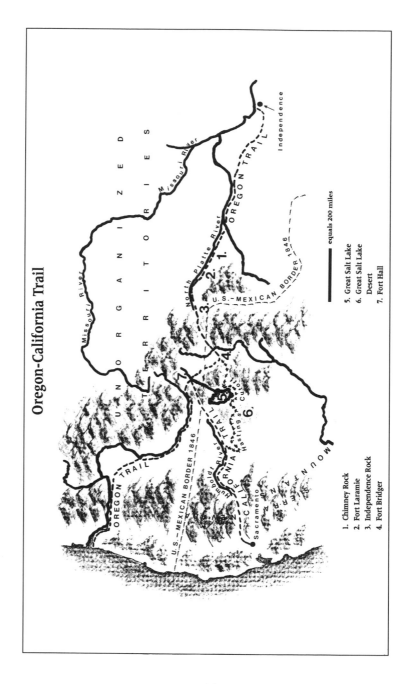

# Oregon-California Trail

**⸻ equals 200 miles**

1. Chimney Rock
2. Fort Laramie
3. Independence Rock
4. Fort Bridger
5. Great Salt Lake
6. Great Salt Lake Desert
7. Fort Hall

be riding in wagons pulled by oxen, and we children were afraid of these animals, thinking they could go wherever they pleased since they had no bridles. At the first bridge we came to, Milt had to stop the wagon and let us out to lighten the load. I remember that I told him to be sure to make the oxen hit the bridge and to remember that Grandma was in the wagon. How he laughed at the idea of the oxen missing the bridge! I soon found that Milt, with his "whoa," "haw," and "gee," could make the oxen do just as he pleased.

The first Indians we met were the Caws, who kept the ferry on the Caw River in Kansas. When they took us across the stream, I watched them closely, hardly daring to draw my breath, feeling sure that they would sink the boat in the middle of the river. I was very thankful when I realized that they were not like Grandma's Indians.

Many in our party rode their horses. Every morning when the wagons were ready to start, Papa and I would jump on our horses, and we would go ahead to pick out a camping spot [for that night]. Mama preferred the wagon, though. She did not like to leave Grandma, although Mama could have done so, since Patty could hardly be persuaded to leave Grandma's side. Our little home was so comfortable that Mama could sit in the wagon, reading and chatting with the little ones, almost forgetting that she was crossing the plains.

Grandma Keyes improved in health and spirits every day until we came to the Big Blue River. This river was so swollen that we could not cross, and we decided to wait

*Opposite: The Oregon-California Trail. Courtesy of Karen Zeinert.*

awhile to see if it would recede. As soon as we stopped traveling, Grandma began to fail, and on the 29th day of May she died. It seemed hard to bury her in the wilderness and travel on. We were also afraid that the Indians would destroy her grave, but nowhere on the whole road could we have found so beautiful a resting place.

By this time, many emigrants had joined our company, and all turned out to assist at the funeral. A coffin was hewn out of a cottonwood tree, and John Denton, a young man from Springfield, found a large gray stone on which he chiseled, "Sarah Keyes, born in Virginia," giving both her age when she died and her date of birth. She was buried under the shade of an oak, the stone being placed at the foot of her grave. We planted wildflowers near the stone. A minister in our party, the Rev. J. A. Cornwall, tried to give words of comfort as we stood about this lonely spot. Strange to say, that grave has never been disturbed. The wilderness blossomed into the city of Manhattan, Kansas, and we have been told that the city cemetery surrounds Grandma's plot.

The river remained high, and there was no prospect of fording it soon. The men then went to work, cutting down trees to make rafts on which to take the wagons over. Logs, about twenty-five feet in length, were tied together. Ropes were attached to the rafts, and they were let out for a crossing and then pulled back to shore to take the next wagon over. The banks of this stream being steep, our heavily laden wagons had to be let down with ropes. Each wagon's wheels were placed in hollowed-out

*In 1866, William Henry Jackson became a driver for a freight wagon train and drove wagons to California on the Oregon Trail. Along the way, Jackson made sketches of many landmarks, such as Chimney Rock, which is pictured here. Later he used these sketches for reference when he painted his now-famous illustrations of the West. Many of his paintings are on permanent display at Scotts Bluff National Monument in Nebraska. Courtesy of Scotts Bluff National Monument.*

spots on the rafts to keep the wagons from rolling off the raft during the crossing. One by one, the wagons were put aboard the rafts. Finally, the difficult work was accomplished, and we resumed our journey.

At first the road was rough, but after striking the great valley of the Platte River, the road was good and the country was beautiful. Stretching out before us as far as the eye could reach was a valley as green as emerald, dotted here and there with flowers of every imaginable color, and through this valley flowed the grand old Platte, a wide, shallow river.

Our company now numbered about forty wagons. For a time, we were commanded by Col. William H. Russell, then by George Donner.

Exercise in the open air under bright skies and freedom from peril combined to make this part of our journey an ideal pleasure trip. How I enjoyed riding my pony, galloping over the plains, gathering wildflowers! At night the young folks would gather about the campfire, chatting merrily. Often a song would be heard or some clever dancer would lower the hind gate of a wagon and do a jig on it.

Traveling up the smooth valley of the Platte, we passed Court House Rock, Chimney Rock, and Scotts Bluff. We made from fifteen to twenty miles a day, shortening or lengthening the distance in order to secure a good camping ground.

At night when we drove into camp, our wagons were placed so as to form a circle or corral into which our cattle were driven after grazing to prevent the Indians from stealing them. The campfires and tents were on the outside.

There were many expert riflemen in the party, and we never lacked for game. The plains were alive with buffalo, and herds could be seen every day coming to the Platte to drink. The meat of the young buffalo is excellent and so is that of the antelope. However, the antelope were so fleet of foot, it was difficult to get a shot at one.

I witnessed many a buffalo hunt and more than once was in the chase close beside my father. When a buffalo sees a hunter, he raises his shaggy head, gazes at him for a moment, then turns and runs. A buffalo will not attack unless wounded, and then he is very dangerous. For this reason, it is very important to fell the animal immediately. The only other danger lay in a stampede, for nothing could withstand the onward rush of these massive creatures whose tread seemed to shake the whole prairie.

# Within Minutes There Were
# Three Bulls Coming Toward Me

*James F. Reed*

South Fork of the Platte River
[Nebraska Territory]
ten miles from the crossing
Tuesday, June 16, 1846

Dear Brother,

Today, seven men from Oregon, who went out last year, passed through our camp on the way back to the States. One is well acquainted with our relative, Caden Keyes. These men met an advance Oregon caravan about 150 miles west of Fort Laramie and counted 478 wagons bound for California or Oregon. There are forty wagons in our train, which makes 518 in all. It is said that there are twenty behind us.

*James Reed and others found sport in hunting buffalo, which were an important source of food for pioneers crossing the plains. Courtesy of the Dover Pictorial Archives.*

Tomorrow we cross the river, and by our reckoning, we will be two hundred miles from Fort Laramie, where we intend to stop to repair our wagon wheels. They are all loose, and I will stop sooner if I can find enough wood. There is no wood here, and our women and children gather buffalo chips for fires so they can cook. These chips [dried buffalo manure] burn well.

As far as I am concerned, my family affairs go smoothly, and I have nothing to do but hunt, which I have done with great success. My first chance was on the 12th of June, when I returned to camp with a splendid two-year-old elk, the only one killed by anyone in our caravan as yet. I picked the elk out of eight of the biggest I ever beheld, and I really do believe that there were some in the herd as large as the horse I rode.

I also saw my first buffalo hunt. The men who participated are considered the best hunters on the road. Believing that my horse, Glaucus, could beat any horse that I saw used in the hunt, I decided that I could beat the experienced hunters.

Yesterday I decided to try my luck. The old buffalo hunters and as many others as they would permit to be in their company set out from camp for a hunt. Hiram Miller, myself, and two others, after due preparation, took to the line of march. Before we left, everyone in camp was anticipating some choice buffalo meat.

After riding about eight miles, we saw a large herd of buffalo bulls. However, we wanted younger animals with more tender meat. Nevertheless, we went toward the bulls as coolly and calmly as the nature of the chase would permit. As perfectly green as I was, I was chosen to charge into the herd first, cut a few bulls from it, and try to bring one down. Eager to prove myself, I was soon in the midst of the animals. I dashed among them with a Craddock's pistol in hand—a fine instrument for buffalo hunters—selected my victim and brought him tumbling to the ground.

The plains now appeared to be one living, moving mass of bulls, cows, and calves. The latter took my eye, and leaving my companions behind, I again took a spur to Glaucus. I soon found myself among many bulls, which stood between me and the cows and calves, trying to protect them.

Now I thought that the time had arrived to make one bold effort to single out a calf, which I did by dashing into the herd at right angles. It was an exciting time, being in the midst of a herd of upwards of a hundred head of buffalo and entirely out of sight of my companions and completely on my own. At last, after several charges, I succeeded in momentarily separating a calf from the rest of the animals, but within minutes there were three bulls coming toward me. I then charged toward the bulls, separating them. Now I had one bull, which would weigh about twelve hundred pounds, and a fine large calf in my sights, and I set out to claim my prize. I tried as hard as I could to separate the calf from the bull, but no matter how I attempted to get to the calf, the bull would immediately put himself between us. Finding I could not separate them respectfully, I shot the bull.

Then I went after the calf. Time was very important

now, as I had to kill the calf before it reached the safety of the herd. I rode up the hill at full speed, loading my empty pistol as I raced along. When I got close enough, I managed to shoot the calf, and the exciting race ended. I then sat by my trophy and waited for help. Meanwhile, I counted 597 buffalo within sight.

After a while, Miller and one of the others came. They wanted to get a buffalo, too, and I pointed out a few old bulls nearby. I joined in the chase, and after accompanying the men to a height where I could witness the hunt, I stopped. The others put out at full speed. They singled out a large bull, and I do not recollect ever having laughed more than I did at the hunt the boys made. Their horses would do very well at a proper distance from the bull, but as they approached the buffalo, the horses would come to a complete stop about forty yards short of the bull. Eventually, I went forward at full speed and shot the buffalo for them.

Glaucus and I then stayed beside the buffalo until all the hunters had arrived. Glaucus was uncomfortable about being so near the bull, but she obeyed orders. When the others arrived, their horses would not go near the buffalo, even though it was dead.

We secured as much of the meat as we could carry. I was now a successful buffalo hunter, and Glaucus, after careful examination, was pronounced the finest nag in the caravan.

I plan to hunt buffalo again very soon. My wife will accompany me on the next hunt, which is to come off in a few days.

The face of the country here is very hilly even though it has the name of plains.

The weather is rather warm. The thermometer ranges as high as 90° F. during the middle of the day. However, at night temperatures may dip to 45° F.

Our teams are getting on fine so far. Most of the emigrants ahead have lost some horses or oxen due to exhaustion. We have been told that the grass is much better this year throughout the whole route than it was last year.

Tomorrow we move on.

Respectfully,

James F. Reed

# Two Hundred Miles Farther On

## *Virginia Reed Murphy*

We found no trouble in crossing the Platte, the only danger being in quicksand [loose sand and water that can suck down and engulf anything that tries to cross it]. The river was wide, so we had to stop the wagons now and then to give the oxen a few moments' rest.

At Fort Laramie, two hundred miles farther on, we celebrated the Fourth of July in fine style. Camp was pitched earlier than usual, and we prepared a grand dinner. Some of my father's friends in Springfield had given him a bottle of good old brandy. He agreed to drink a toast at a certain hour on this day, looking to the East, while his friends in Illinois were to drink to his success from a companion bottle with their faces turned toward the West. The difference in time was estimated, and at the hour agreed upon, the health of our friends in Springfield was toasted with great enthusiasm.

At Fort Laramie was a party of Sioux, which was on the warpath. It was going to fight the Crows or Blackfeet. The Sioux are fine-looking Indians, and I was not in the least afraid of them. I still had my pony, Billy, then. The Sioux fell in love with him, and they began bargaining for Billy. They brought buffalo robes, beautifully tanned buckskins, pretty beaded moccasins, and ropes made of grass, placing these articles in a heap alongside several of their ponies. By signs, they made my father understand that they would give them all for Billy and me. Papa just smiled and shook his head. Unwilling to give up, the Indians increased the number of ponies, and as a last tempting inducement, they brought an old coat that had been worn by some poor soldier, thinking that my father could not resist the brass buttons. They were greatly disappointed when Papa refused these offerings.

On the sixth of July, we were again on the march. The Sioux were several days in passing our caravan, not on account of the length of our train, but because there were so many Sioux. Owing to the fact that our wagons were strung so far apart, they could have massacred our whole party without much loss to themselves. Some of our company became alarmed, and the rifles were cleaned out and loaded to let the warriors see that we were prepared to fight. But the Sioux never showed any inclination to disturb us.

Their curiosity was annoying, however, and our wagon with its conspicuous stove pipe and mirror attracted their attention. They were continually swarming about, trying to get a look at themselves in the mirror, and

30

*The Donner wagon train encountered many Indians on its way to Cali-
fornia. The Sioux Indians, whose appearance impressed Virginia at Fort
Laramie, are pictured here. Courtesy of the Rare Books and Manuscripts
Division, The New York Public Library, Astor, Lenox and Tilden Foun-
dations.*

*Opposite: This is the earliest known photograph of Fort Laramie, taken
in 1858. It was here that the emigrants celebrated July 4, 1846. Courtesy of the Library of Congress.*

their desire to possess my pony was so strong that at last I had to ride in the wagon and let one of the drivers take charge of Billy. This I did not like.

In order to see how far back the line of warriors went, I picked up a large field glass that hung on a rack, and I quickly extended the tubes on the telescope, making a loud clicking noise as I did so. The sight of the telescope that grew larger in only a few seconds and the strange noise frightened the warriors. They jumped back, wheeled their ponies about, and scattered. This pleased me greatly, and I told my mother that I could fight the whole Sioux tribe with a spyglass. Whenever they came near to get a peep at their war paint and feathers in the mirror, I would raise the glass as revenge for forcing me to ride in the wagon. I loved to see them dart away in terror, and I laughed as they ran from me.

A new route had just been opened by Lansford W. Hastings. Called the Hastings Cutoff, this trail passed along the southern shore of the Great Salt Lake, and then it rejoined the old Fort Hall emigrant road on the Humboldt River. It was said to shorten the distance three hundred miles. Much time was lost in debating which course to pursue when we reached Fort Bridger, the turning off spot. [Legendary mountain man Jim] Bridger and [his partner Louis] Vasquez, who were in charge of the fort, sounded the praises of the new road. My father was so eager to reach California that he was quick to take advantage of any means to shorten the distance, and he decided to take the cutoff.

# A Better Route

*James F. Reed*

Fort Bridger
[Southwestern Wyoming]
July 31, 1846

Dear Brother,

We have arrived here safely with only the loss of two yoke of my best oxen. They were poisoned by drinking water in a little creek called the Dry Sandy, located between the Great Spring and the Little Sandy. Jacob Donner also lost two yoke, and George Donner lost a yoke and a half, all supposedly from the same cause. I have replenished my stock by purchasing some from Mr. Vasquez and Mr. Bridger, two very excellent and accommodating gentlemen who run this fort.

A new road, the Hastings Cutoff, leaves the Fort Hall road here. It is said to be a savings of 350 or 400 miles in going to California and a better route. There is, however, thought to be one stretch of forty miles without water. But Hastings and his party are out ahead, examining

*Fort Bridger was established as a trading post by Jim Bridger in 1843. This fort was located in what is now southeastern Wyoming. Courtesy of the Dover Pictorial Archives.*

sources for water or a way to bypass this portion of the trail. I think that they cannot avoid a long, dry stretch, for the trail crosses an arm of the Eutaw [Utah] Lake. However, Mr. Bridger and other gentlemen here, who have trapped that country, say that the lake has receded from the tract in question, and this would make the trek shorter. There is plenty of grass, which we can cut and put into the wagons for our cattle to eat while we cross the forty-mile stretch.

Mr. Bridger informs me that the route we mean to take is a fine, level road with plenty of water and grass, with the exception mentioned before. It is estimated that seven hundred miles will take us to Captain Sutter's Fort [near Sacramento], which we hope to make in seven weeks from this day.

We are now only one hundred miles from the Great Salt Lake by the new route. On this route, we will not have dust since there are but sixty wagons ahead of us. The rest of the train will go the long route, feeling afraid of the cutoff.

I want you to inform any emigrants heading this way that they can be supplied with fresh cattle by Mr. Vasquez and Mr. Bridger. They have now about two hundred head of oxen, cows, and young cattle with a great many horses and mules. They can also be relied on for doing business honorably and fairly. Mr. Bridger will go to St. Louis this fall, and he plans to return with emigrants in the spring. He will be very useful as a guide.

I have fine times in hunting grouse, antelope, or mountain goats, which are plentiful. Milt Elliott, James Smith, and Walter Herron, the young men who drive for me, are careful, first-rate drivers, which gives me time for hunting. We are beyond the range of buffalo.

The independent trappers, who swarm here during the passing of the emigrants, are as great a set of sharks as ever disgraced humanity, with few exceptions. Let the emigrants avoid trading with them. Vasquez and Bridger are the only fair traders in these parts.

There are two gentlemen here, an Englishman named Wills and a Yankee named Miles, who will leave here in a few days to settle at some favorable point on the

*Jim Bridger was a legendary mountain man. A fur trapper and a guide, he was one of the first white men in what is now Wyoming and Utah. When he was driven out of Fort Bridger by the Mormons in 1853, he worked as a guide again, leading government expeditions to the Yellowstone and Powder River areas. Courtesy of the National Archives.*

Salt Lake. In a short time, it will be a fine place for emigrants to recruit teams by exchanging broken-down oxen for good teams.

Respectfully,
James F. Reed

# The Hastings Cutoff

*Virginia Reed Murphy*

None of our party knew then, as we learned afterwards, that Bridger and Vasquez worked for Hastings, and as such, they had a financial interest in seeing that the new route prospered. None of us knew then, either, that Papa's friend, Mr. Bryant, who had left the train and gone ahead on his own, had left a letter at the fort warning us not to take the cutoff, a letter Bridger and Vasquez never delivered. But for the advice of these men, we should have continued on the old Fort Hall road with the others. Instead, seventy-four of us decided to take the Hastings Cutoff.

On the morning of July 31, we parted with our traveling companions, some of whom had become very dear friends. Without any suspicion of impending disaster, we set off in high spirits. But a few days on the road proved that the cutoff was not as it had been represented. This road had not been well marked or worn smooth by hundreds of wagons as our old trail had been. Instead, at times it was hard to find any trace of the cutoff.

*Emigrants on their way to California traveled over narrow and very steep trails when they reached mountains. Because many teams of oxen had to be used on occasion to pull one wagon, few emigrants braved the journey on their own. This was true even thirty years after the Donners went west. This photo of a large train was probably taken in the 1870s (note the telegraph poles). Courtesy of the National Archives.*

Nevertheless, we made reasonably good time, and seven days later we reached Weber Canyon. Here we received shocking news. Hastings, who was guiding a party in advance of ours, left a note warning us that the low road through the canyon was impassable for all but the smallest wagons. It was too late to turn back, for we were already far behind schedule and every day now brought

# Hastings Cutoff Wagon Train
*Left Fort Bridger on July 31, 1846*
*(ages of members given in parentheses)*

*The James Reed group—three wagons*
Same as before, except for the loss of Grandma Keyes

*The Donner group—six wagons*
The original Springfield group minus Hiram Miller, who refused to take the cutoff. Additions who joined the party somewhere along the trail: Charles T. Stanton (35), from Chicago; Luke Halloran (25), an invalid from Missouri; Antonio (23), a herder from New Mexico; and Jean Baptiste Trubode (23), a driver hired to replace Hiram Miller

*The Breen–Dolan group from Keokuk, Iowa—four wagons*
Patrick (40) and Margaret (40) Breen
Their children: John (14), Edward (13), Patrick, Jr. (11), Simon (9), Peter (7), James (4), and Isabella (1)
A friend: Patrick Dolan (40)

*The Eddy group from Belleville, Illinois—one wagon*
William H. (28) and Eleanor (25) Eddy
Their children: James (3) and Margaret (1)

*The Keseberg group from Germany—two wagons*
Louis (32) and Philippine (23) Keseberg
Their children: Ada (3) and Louis, Jr. (1)
The driver: Karl (?) Burger (30)
A passenger: ———— Hardcoop (60+), an immigrant from Belgium

*The Wolfinger group from Germany—one wagon*
Mr. —— (30?) and Mrs. —— (25?) Wolfinger

*The Spitzer and Reinhardt group from Germany—one wagon*
Augustus Spitzer (30) and Joseph Reinhardt (30)

*The McCutchen group from Missouri—no wagon, rode with others*
William (30) and Amanda (24) McCutchen
Their daughter: Harriet (1)

*The Murphy-Foster-Pike group from Tennessee and
Missouri—two wagons*
Lavina Murphy (50)
Lavina's five children: Landrum (15), Mary (13),
Lemuel (12), William (11), and Simon (10)
Lavina's married daughter and son-in-law: Sarah (23)
and William (28) Foster,
The Fosters' son: George (4)
Lavina's other married daughter and son-in-law:
Harriet (21) and William M. (25) Pike
The Pikes' daughters: Naomi (3) and Catherine (1)

*The Graves–Fosdick group from Illinois—three wagons*
Franklin, Sr. (57), and Elizabeth (47) Graves
Their children: Mary (20), William (18), Eleanor (15),
Lovina (13), Nancy (9), Jonathan (7), Franklin Ward,
Jr. (5), and Elizabeth (1)
The Graves's married daughter and son-in-law: Sarah
(22?) and Jay (23) Fosdick

the threat of getting snowbound in the Sierra Nevada Mountains. Hastings advised us to take another way to the Salt Lake through the Wasatch Mountains, the path of which he attempted to give on paper.

These directions were so vague that C. T. Stanton, William Pike, and my father went to find Hastings to seek his help. After an exhausting journey upon which they saw firsthand the narrow canyon filled with huge boulders and dangerous ledges, they finally found Hastings. They tried to persuade him to return to guide our party. Hastings refused to do so, but he came back over a portion of the road, and from a high mountain, he tried to point out the general course.

Stanton, Pike, and the men's horses were too exhausted to return to the wagon train immediately. They rested while my father, on a horse he borrowed from Hastings, traveled alone on the route Hastings had recommended. My father took notes and blazed trees to assist him in retracing his course. He reached camp five days after he left Hastings.

After learning of the hardships of the advance train from my father, our party decided to abandon any hope of going through Weber Canyon. Instead, we decided to push our way through an uncharted wilderness. Only those who have passed through this country on horseback can appreciate our situation. There was absolutely no road, not even a trail. Trees and heavy underbrush had to be cut down in the canyons to make a path. It was exhausting, backbreaking work that fell to less than half of the party. We had only twenty-seven men among us, and several were too old or too weak to build roads. It took the men six days to clear a trail only thirteen miles in length.

While cutting our way step by step, we were overtaken and joined by the Graves group: W. F. Graves; his wife; their eight children; the Graves's son-in-law, Jay Fosdick; and a young man by the name of John Snyder. This brought our number to eighty-seven.

After many days of grueling work, we reached a point where it looked as though our wagons would have to be abandoned. We had to go over a high ridge, and it seemed impossible for the oxen to pull them up the steep hill. Still we decided to give it a try. The oxen were brought to the foot of the hill, and almost every yoke in the whole train was required to pull up one wagon, then lower it on the other side. It was slow work, but at last it was accomplished, and we had finally worked our way through the Wasatch Mountains.

While we were pulling the wagons over the ridge, Stanton and Pike rejoined us.

Worn with travel and greatly discouraged, we finally reached the shore of the Great Salt Lake. The cutoff had taken an entire month instead of the one week that Hastings had estimated, and our cattle were so exhausted that they were not fit to cross the desert.

We encamped in a valley called Twenty Wells. The water in these wells was pure and cold, welcome enough after the alkaline pools from which we had been forced to drink. After a brief rest, we prepared for the forced march across the desert and laid in, as we supposed, an ample supply of water and grass.

The desert had been represented to us as only forty

miles wide, but we found it nearer eighty. It was a dreary, desolate, alkali waste, and not a living thing could be seen. It seemed as though the hand of death had been laid upon the country. We started in the evening, traveled all that night and all the following day and night—two nights and one day of suffering from thirst and heat by day and piercing cold by night. [Although we made progress the second day,] when the third night fell, we still saw the barren waste stretching away, apparently as boundless as when we started. We were not prepared for such a lengthy stretch, and we had but a few drops of water left now.

My father decided to go ahead in search of water. Before starting, he instructed our drivers to take the oxen from the wagons, and the cattle as well, if they showed signs of giving out and follow him. He had not been gone long before the oxen began to fall to the ground from thirst and exhaustion. They, and many others, were unhitched at once and driven ahead. My father met the drivers with the cattle when he was coming back. He instructed the men to go to the water, which was about ten miles away, then return as soon as the animals had satisfied their thirst. Papa reached us about daylight.

We waited all that day in the desert, looking for the return of our drivers. The other wagons, eventually going on without us, disappeared out of sight. Towards night, the situation became desperate. Another day without water meant death.

We had no choice but to set out on foot and try to reach some of the other wagons. I can never forget that night in the desert. We walked mile after mile in the dark-

*Keeping livestock—especially oxen—alive and healthy was a premier task for emigrants. Without these beasts they were at the mercy of the elements and the Indians. This illustration is by Frederic Remington, a now-famous artist who traveled throughout the West, drawing pictures of what he saw.*

ness, every step seeming to be the very last we could take.

Suddenly all fatigue was banished by fear! Through the night came a swift rushing sound of one of the young steers, which was crazed by thirst and apparently bent upon our destruction. My father, holding his youngest child in his arms and keeping us all close behind him, drew his pistol. We waited for the attack, but finally the maddened beast turned and dashed off into the darkness.

Dragging ourselves along, we finally reached the wagon of Jacob Donner. The family was asleep, so we quietly lay down on the ground. A bitter wind swept over the desert, chilling us through and through, and we crept closer together to try to get warm. When we complained of the cold, Papa placed all five of our dogs around us, and only the warmth of these faithful creatures kept us from perishing.

At daylight, Papa was off to learn the fate of his cattle. He was told that all were lost, except one cow and an ox. The stock, scenting the water, had rushed on ahead of the men. Because the animals hadn't been seen since they escaped, the drivers assumed that the cattle had been rounded up by Indians and driven into the mountains.

Hoping that the animals still might be recovered, we decided to make a diligent search. Almost every man in the company turned out, hunting in all directions for a week for our animals as well as many others that had also escaped when loosened from their yokes. Our eighteen head of cattle and oxen were never found. We were eight hundred miles from California, seemingly helpless, for our wagons had to be abandoned.

*Captain John A. Sutter was born in Switzerland in 1803, and emigrated to America in 1834. Sutter lived in Missouri, New Mexico, and Oregon before settling in California. He received large land grants from the Mexican government in California, where he set up a small colony. Sutter prospered and gladly shared his wealth with needy Americans who moved into the area. Courtesy of the California State Department of Parks, Sutter's Fort State Historic Park.*

The company then met and kindly agreed to let us have two yoke of oxen. These animals, yoked with our one remaining ox and cow, would make it possible for us to pull one small wagon. We filled it with only the most basic necessities. Our extra food was distributed among the other wagons, and those transporting our food insisted on being able to use it if necessary.

Some of the company went back with Papa and assisted him in caching belongings that could not be packed in the wagon. A cache is made by digging a hole in the ground. A box or the bed of a wagon is placed in the hole, and articles to be left behind are put into this box, which is covered first with boards, then dirt. Thus the goods are hidden from sight, safe until their owner could return for them sometime in the future. Our smallest wagon was used to cache our goods; our two-story palace car was simply abandoned.

Before leaving the desert camp, an inventory of food was taken, and it was found that the supply was not sufficient to last us all the way to California. We decided that someone must go on to Sutter's Fort near Sacramento for provisions, and a call was made for volunteers. C. T. Stanton and William McCutchen bravely offered their services and started out immediately, bearing letters from the company to Captain Sutter asking for relief.

As if to render the situation even more terrible, a storm came on during the night, and the hilltops became white with snow. Our confidence shaken, we looked at the snow with fearful foreboding before resuming our journey.

# Tragedy

*Virginia Reed Murphy*

On October 5, shortly after we had reached the Humboldt River on the old Fort Hall Trail, a tragedy was enacted which affected the future lives and fortunes of more than one member of our company. This tragedy began when we were compelled to double our teams in order to ascend a steep hill. Milt Elliott, who was driving our wagon, and John Snyder, who was driving one of Mr. Graves's wagons, became involved in a quarrel over how best to reach the summit and the management of their oxen.

Snyder continued to struggle with his team his own way, but his oxen were unable to pull the wagon over the difficult trail. Angry and frustrated, Snyder beat his cattle with the butt end of his whip. My father witnessed this scene. Papa was well aware of the great importance of saving the remainder of the oxen, and he tried to reason with Snyder, reminding him how dependent we were on the remaining animals. To ease Snyder's problems, Papa offered the assistance of our team.

Snyder, already angered by something Milt had said, declared that his team could pull up alone, and he began using abusive language. Father tried to quiet the enraged man, and hard words followed. Papa then tried to calm Snyder by saying, "We can settle this, John, when we get up the hill."

"No," Snyder replied, with an oath, "we will settle it now." After springing upon the tongue of the wagon, he gave my father a violent blow over the head with his whip. Another blow followed, then another!

Father was stunned for a moment and blinded by the blood that was streaming from the gashes in his head. When Snyder struck again, my mother ran between the men. Father saw Mother coming and the uplifted whip, and he cried out, "John, John!" But it was too late. The stroke came down upon my mother. Quick as a thought, my father's hunting knife was out, and a moment later, Snyder had been fatally wounded.

By now, others had rushed to the scene. As Snyder fell backwards, he was caught in the arms of William Graves and laid on the ground.

My father regretted the act, and wiping the blood from his eyes, he went quickly to the assistance of the dying man. I can see him now as he knelt over Snyder, trying to stanch the wound, while the blood from his gashes, trickling down his face, mingled with that of the dying man. A few moments later, Snyder died.

Camp was pitched immediately, our wagon being some distance from the others. Father then came to me and said, "Daughter, do you think you can dress these wounds in my head? Your mother is not able, and they must be attended to."

I answered that I thought I could, if he would tell me what to do. I brought a basin of water and a sponge, and we went into the wagon so that we might not be disturbed. When my work was at last finished, I burst out crying.

Papa clasped me in his arms, saying, "I should not have asked so much of you." He held me and talked to me until I could control my emotions to such a degree that I could go to the tent where Mama was lying and not upset her.

My father was eager to do what he could for Snyder. Papa offered the boards of our wagon from which to make a coffin. At the funeral he stood sorrowfully by until the last clod was placed upon the grave. He and John Snyder had been good friends, and no one could have regretted the taking of that young life more than my father.

The members of the Donner party decided to hold a council meeting to determine my father's fate. At the meeting, the members refused to accept Papa's pleas of self-defense. The feeling against my father at one time was so strong that lynching was proposed. He was no coward, and he bared his neck, saying, "Come on, gentlemen," but no one moved.

I believe that all the animosity towards my father was caused by Louis Keseberg, a German who had joined our company back on the plains. Keseberg was married to a young, pretty German girl, and he was in the habit of beating her until she was black and blue. This aroused all the manhood in my father, and he took Keseberg to task, telling him that the beating must be stopped. Keseberg did not dare to strike his wife again, but he hated my father and nursed his wrath. When Papa killed Snyder, Keseberg's hour for revenge had come. But how a man like Keseberg, brutal and overbearing, although highly educated, could have had such influence over the company is more than I can understand.

Eventually, the company decided to send Papa into the wilderness to die of slow starvation or to be murdered by the Indians. When the sentence of banishment was announced, my father refused to go, feeling that he was justified in what he had done.

Then came a sacrifice on the part of my mother. Knowing only too well how difficult her life would be without him, yet convinced that if he remained, he would meet with violence at the hands of his enemies, she implored him to go. Papa refused to change his mind until Mama urged him to remember the destitution of the company, saying that if he remained he might see his children starve to death and be helpless to aid them. On the other hand, she argued, if he went on, he could find food at Sutter's Fort and return with it for them. It was a fearful struggle. At last he consented, but not before he had secured a promise from the company to care for his wife and little ones.

My father was sent out into an unknown country without food or arms. When I learned about this, I slipped away after dark, taking Milt with me. Following the old trail, we took a rifle, pistols, ammunition, and some food to Papa. I had decided to stay with him, and I begged him to let me do so. But he would not listen to my arguments,

*The Donner party went through several deserts. The first, which Virginia describes, was flat and hard, with little vegetation. Another desert, in western Nevada, not mentioned by Virginia, is pictured above in a photograph taken by a survey team in 1867. Parts of this desert, referred to by some of the emigrants as "the dunes," were covered by powdery sand that was so fine it resembled ashes. As a result, oxen struggled to pull their wagons, and drivers' tempers flared often as the wagons became mired in the sand. Courtesy of the National Archives.*

saying only that it was impossible. Finally, unclasping my arms from around him, he told Milt to take care of me, and shortly after, we started back to our camp. I cried so hard that I barely had strength to walk.

When we reached the camp, I saw the distress of my mother with the little ones clinging around her and no Papa to lean upon. This scene made a woman of me, for I realized that I had to be strong and help Mama bear her sorrows.

The Donners were not with us when my father was banished. Instead, they were several days in advance of our train. Walter Herron, one of our former drivers, traveled with the Donners after we had to abandon two of our wagons in the desert. When Papa overtook the Donners, Herron decided to leave the train and accompany my father.

We traveled on, but all life seemed to have left the party. Every day, we would search for some sign of Papa. Sometimes he would leave a letter by the wayside in the top of a bush or in a split stick, and when he succeeded in killing geese or birds, he would scatter the feathers about so that we might know that he was not suffering for food. When possible, our fire would always be kindled on the spot where his had been. But a time came when we found no letter and no trace of him.

My mother's despair was pitiful. [My sister] Patty and I thought that we would lose her also. But life and energy were again aroused in her by the danger that her children would starve. It was apparent that the whole company would soon be put on a short allowance [limited portions] of food.

Our wagon soon became too heavy for our terribly weak animals, and it was abandoned along with everything we could spare. Our remaining things were packed in part of another family's wagon. We had two horses left, which could hardly drag themselves along, but they managed to carry my two little brothers. The rest of us had to walk, one of us going beside the horse that carried my youngest brother to hold him on his mount.

On October 19, while traveling along the Truckee River, our hearts were gladdened by the return of Stanton. He brought seven mules loaded with provisions that he had obtained at Sutter's Fort. Mr. McCutchen, who had left with him, was too weak to travel, but Captain Sutter had sent two of his Indian herdsmen, Luis and Salvador, with Stanton to help us.

Hungry as we were, Stanton brought us something better than food—news. He had seen Papa. Stanton had met him not far from Sutter's Fort. Papa had been three days without food and his horse was not able to carry him, but he was still alive! Stanton had given him a horse and some provisions, and he had headed off to the fort.

We now packed what little we had left on one mule and started with Stanton. Mother rode on a mule, carrying my youngest brother on her lap. Patty and Jimmy rode behind the two Indians, and I rode behind Stanton. In this way we journeyed on, looking up with fear towards the mountains, our last barrier, where snow was already falling even though it was only the last week in October. Winter had set in a month earlier than usual. All trails and roads were covered with snow, and our only guide was the sight of the summit, which it seemed we could never reach. Despair drove many nearly frantic.

Each family tried to cross the summit, but found it impossible. When it was seen that the wagons could not be dragged through the snow, they were abandoned and their goods and provisions were packed on oxen for a second attempt. Men and women, walking in the snow up to their waists, carried their children in their arms and tried to drive their cattle at the same time. Everyone tired quickly, and we had to stop to rest often.

While we rested, Stanton went ahead to scout the trail. He came back several hours later and reported that we could get across if we kept right on, but that it would be impossible if more snow fell. He was in favor of a forced march. But some in our party were so exhausted by the day's labor that they declared that they could not take another step. So the few who knew the danger that the night might bring yielded to the many, and we camped within three miles of the summit.

That night the dreaded snow came. The air was so full of great feathery flakes that one could see objects only a few feet away. The Indians knew we were doomed, and one of them wrapped his blanket about him and stood under a tree all night. We children slept on our cold bed of snow with a white mantle falling over us so thickly that every few moments my mother would have to shake the shawl over us to keep us from being buried.

In the morning, the snow lay deep everywhere. We were snowbound in the Sierras.

# Part Two

*Overleaf: Approaching storm. Courtesy of John A. Zeinert.*

# Editor's Note

*Three new sources appear in Part II. Excerpts, or parts, of Patrick Breen's diary have been included to give readers a more detailed account of what life was like in the Sierras for the Donner party during the winter of 1846–47. Breen began his diary about a month after the party became snowbound. He described the weather in detail and listed deaths as he learned about them, events that Virginia does not mention in her account. Also, Breen recorded several incidents involving the Reeds, which Virginia omitted. These entries were written from firsthand observations. The Breens took in the Reeds when Virginia's family needed shelter in the mountains. Breen's excerpts appear under his own byline.*

*Virginia's father had little opportunity to send letters to friends in Illinois immediately after he was exiled from the wagon train. So, his account in Part II is told through excerpts from two new sources, a newspaper article and passages from his diary, which was started in February 1847.*

*The article, "Narrative of the Suffering of a Company of Emigrants in the Mountains of California in the Winter of 1846– 47," describes Reed's life-and-death struggle after he left the wagon train. Reed made many notes about his experiences afterward, and these notes were used by a reporter, J. H. Merryman.*

*Merryman's account appeared in many newspapers of the day, including the* Illinois Journal *on December 9, 1847.*

*Excerpts from James Reed's diary recorded Reed's efforts to help the Donner party when he learned that the wagon train was stranded in the mountains. Although Reed tried to write little beyond the bare facts, at times he was overcome with emotion, and his fear and anguish come through in several passages.*

*Both the Breen and Reed diaries were written for the same reasons: The accounts would explain what had happened in case everyone died, and they would help identify the bodies should they ever be discovered. The diaries were sometimes written in haste and under very trying circumstances. Some of Reed's diary, for example, was written while he huddled near a fire in a blinding snowstorm. Needless to say, correct spelling and perfect punctuation were not of the greatest importance. Misspellings have been corrected, and a few words and punctuation marks have been added to make the passages more readable. On the whole, though, the excerpts are essentially the same as they were when they were written more than 150 years ago: incomplete sentences and fragments, prose written by men who were facing death.*

*K. Z.*

# Chronology

November 4, 1846    After an unsuccessful second attempt to cross the summit, the party decides to set up a winter camp at Donner Lake. All stay here except the Donner group, which sets up camp in Alder Creek valley, five miles away.

November 20    Patrick Breen starts his diary.

November 21–22    Stanton and 21 others set out to cross the summit to get help. They are unable to get through the snow and return to camp.

Late November    James Smith dies. This is the first death at Alder Creek.

December 16, 1846–    A group known as the "Forlorn Hope,"
January 18, 1847    15 members of the wagon train, put on snowshoes and start out for Sutter's Fort. Baylis Williams dies. This is the first death at Donner Lake.

December 25    Mrs. Reed brings out scraps of food hidden away for many weeks for a special Christmas dinner.

January 4–8, 1847    Mrs. Reed attempts to cross the summit with Virginia, the hired girl Eliza, and Milt Elliott in order to get food for her children. The group spends five days in the mountains before being forced to return to the lake.

January 10     When the Reeds' cabin becomes unfit, they are taken in by the Breen family.

December 1846–February 3, 1847     James Reed goes to southern California seeking aid for the wagon train. He is told that no help can be spared because all available men are driving the Mexicans out of California. Reed volunteers to fight, hoping that the conflict in the area will end soon and then someone will help him. When the Mexicans in the area are defeated, local volunteer groups, like Reed's, disband. Now attention is turned to the plight of the emigrants in the mountains. More than $1,300 is raised in San Francisco for provisions. Supplies are put under the charge of S. E. Woodworth, who is to deliver them by boat to the mouth of the Feather River. When the boat does not arrive on schedule, Reed and McCutchen go to Johnson's, where they receive other provisions. They head off for Donner Lake, leaving word for Woodworth to follow them as soon as possible.

February 5–18     Sutter's rescue party goes to Donner Lake after William Eddy arrives at Sutter's Fort, giving both the party's location and a report about the extreme suffering at the lake. Eddy is one of seven survivors of the "Forlorn Hope" group. The other six are at Johnson's, too weak to go on to Sutter's Fort. The rescuers are shocked and appalled by what they find when they reach the winter camp.

| | |
|---|---|
| February 9 | Milt Elliott dies and is buried in the snow by Virginia and Mrs. Reed. |
| February 22–27 | The Reed family, along with 18 others, goes to the Bear River valley with Sutter's rescuers. Glover takes Patty and Tommy Reed back to the lake camp when they prove to be too weak to make the strenuous journey. |
| February 27 | Mrs. Reed and others with the first rescue party meet James Reed and the second rescue party. After an emotional reunion, Mr. Reed continues on to Donner Lake with provisions while his wife and the others descend on to Sutter's Fort. |
| March 1 | James Reed and ten men arrive at Donner Lake and distribute supplies. |
| March 3 | Reed leaves Donner Lake with 17 people bound for Sutter's Fort. |
| March 6–8 | Reed's party is snowbound. |
| March 10 | Some of Reed's party stumbles into Woodworth's camp. A third rescue party leaves Woodworth's camp to bring in survivors from Reeds' party left along the trail as well as anyone able to walk out from Donner Lake. |
| April 13–17 | A fourth rescue team goes to Donner Lake and finds only Louis Keseberg alive. Of the 83 emigrants who were snowbound, 42 had perished. Only 18 of the 32 original Donner party members from Springfield survived to reach California. |

# With Heavy Hearts

*Virginia Reed Murphy*

After failing to cross the summit, we turned around with heavy hearts, abandoning our wagons, plodding along on foot until we reached a cabin that had been built by the Murphy–Schallenberger party two years before. This site, which became the place of death to many in our company, was on the shore of a lake since known as Donner Lake.

The Donners had been behind us. When informed that crossing the mountains was impossible, they decided to stay put in Alder Creek Valley, five miles below the lake. They were, if possible, in a worse condition than ourselves. We at least had the old building. The Donners were forced to live in shelters made mostly from brush topped with pine boughs.

When the first storm ended, we prepared the best we could to try to survive the winter. The men built two double shelters, which were known as the Murphy–Eddy

*The main body of the Donner wagon train spent the winter of 1846–47 on the shores of Donner Lake. At first the lake was a source of fish and water. However, once the lake froze over and was buried beneath more than ten feet of snow, it was of little use to the emigrants. Courtesy of the Library of Congress.*

cabin and the Reed–Graves cabin. They also repaired the roof of the Murphy–Schallenberger building, where the Breens decided to live. Keseberg added a lean-to to this shelter for his family. Mrs. McCutchen and her baby stayed with the Graves family, and Stanton and the two Indians made their home with us.

Next, most of the cattle were slaughtered, and the meat was buried in the snow for preservation. My mother had no cattle to kill, but she made arrangements for some, promising to give two for one in California. All parts of

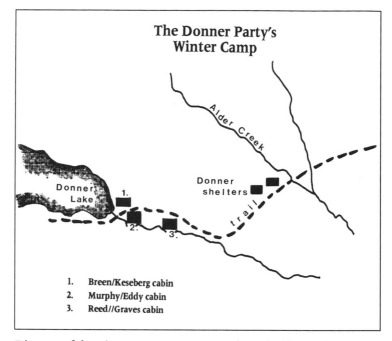

**The Donner Party's Winter Camp**

Donner Lake

Alder Creek

Donner shelters

trail

1.

2.

3.

1. Breen/Keseberg cabin
2. Murphy/Eddy cabin
3. Reed//Graves cabin

*Diagram of the winter camps at Donner Lake and Alder Creek. Courtesy of Karen Zeinert.*

the carcasses were used, even the animals' hides, which were thrown over our roofs to help keep out the snow.

We had little beyond the cattle to eat, and because we feared starvation, some of our members decided to try to cross the mountains to get help from Sutter's Fort. While doing so, they encountered one of the worst winters and the deepest snow ever recorded in the Sierras.

# No Living Thing Without Wings
# Can Get About

*from Patrick Breen's Diary*

November 20—Came to the lake on the 31st of last month. We went on to the pass. Snow was so deep, we were unable to find the road when we were within three miles of the summit. One day after we arrived here, Stanton led our teams and wagons toward the summit again. After an unsuccessful attempt to cross, we returned to the lake. It continued to snow on the mountains for eight days with little intermission. The remainder of the time here, up to this day, was clear and pleasant. Freezing at night.

November 21—Twenty-two of our company are going to try to cross the mountain to get help, including Stanton and the Indians.

November 22—No account from those on the mountains.

November 23—The expedition across the mountains returned after an unsuccessful attempt. Mules couldn't get through the snow.

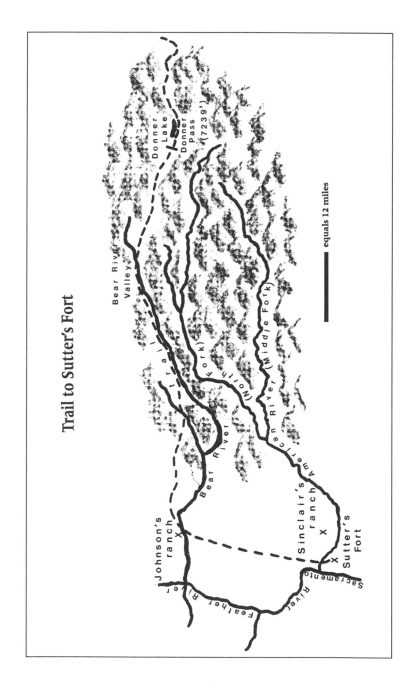

Trail to Sutter's Fort

equals 12 miles

Donner Lake
Donner Pass
(7239')

Bear River Valley

Trail

Bear River (North Fork)

American River (Middle Fork)

Johnson's ranch
X

Sinclair's ranch
X

Sutter's Fort
X

Feather River

Sacramento River

November 25—Cloudy. Looks like the eve of a storm. Our mountaineers intend trying to cross the summit tomorrow if weather permits, without mules. Froze hard last night.

November 26—It began to snow yesterday in the evening. Now it rains or sleets. Wet and muddy. The mountaineers didn't start today.

November 27—Continues to snow. Dull prospects for crossing the mountains.

November 28—Snowing fast.

November 29—Still snowing. Now about three feet deep. Hard to get wood.

November 30—Snowing fast, looks likely to continue. No drifts. Snow is about four or five feet deep. No living thing without wings can get about.

December 1—Still snowing. Snow is almost six feet deep. No going from the house, completely housed up. More snow likely. Stanton's mules wandered off during the night, lost in the snow, no hopes of finding them alive.

December 2—It doesn't snow quite as fast as it did before. Snow must be over six feet deep.

December 3—Snowed a little last night. Today cloudy. Warm, but not warm enough to melt snow lying deep all

*Opposite: The trail over the Sierra Nevada from Donner Lake. It was more than sixty miles to Johnson's ranch, and then another twenty-five or so to Sutter's Fort—a long way to walk for people who were starving and freezing to death. Courtesy of Karen Zeinert.*

around. Began to snow in the afternoon, likely to do so all night.

December 4—Neither snow nor rain this day. It is a relief to have one fine day.

December 6—The morning fine and clear. Now some clouds. Little melting in the sunshine. Stanton and Graves manufacturing snowshoes for another attempt to cross the mountains. No account of mules.

December 9—Commenced snowing before noon. Snows fast.

December 10—Snowed fast all night with heavy squalls of wind. Continues to snow. Don't know the depth, maybe seven feet.

December 11—Snowing a little.

December 12—Continues to snow.

December 13—Snows faster than on any previous day. Snow eight feet deep on the level. Stanton and Graves with several others nearly ready to cross the mountains.

# To Stay Alive

*Virginia Reed Murphy*

On December 16, a group, since known as the "Forlorn Hope," left camp to cross the mountains to seek relief for us and to reduce the number of people in our camp dependent upon so little food. Franklin Graves and Charles Stanton made snowshoes for the trip, and when they were finished, fifteen members of our party—Stanton, Graves, Jay Fosdick, Patrick Dolan, Lemuel Murphy, Antonio, William Eddy, William and Sarah Murphy Foster, Harriet Murphy Pike, Amanda McCutchen, Sarah Graves Fosdick, Mary Graves, plus the two Indians that Sutter sent—started for Sutter's Fort.

While these members struggled toward relief, we struggled to stay alive. The misery endured at Donner Lake in our little dark cabins under the snow could make the coldest heart ache.

Christmas was near, but to most of the starving, its arrival gave no comfort, and it came and passed without much observance. However, my mother had determined weeks before that her children should have a treat on this

71

one day. She had laid away a few dried apples, some beans, a bit of tripe [stomach of an ox] and a small piece of bacon. When this hoarded store was brought out, the delight of the little ones knew no bounds. The cooking was watched carefully, and when we sat down to our Christmas dinner, Mother said, "Children eat slowly, for this one day you can have all you wish." The relief of that one bright day, ending weeks of misery, was a great blessing, and whenever I sit down to a Christmas dinner now, my thoughts go back to that special day at Donner Lake.

The storms would often last ten days at a time. The snowfall was so heavy on occasion that we had to shovel out snow from our fireplaces before a fire could be made in the morning. When the storms were at their worst, we dared not leave our shelters, and we had to cut chips from the walls of our log cabins for fuel.

The beef we had slaughtered was buried beneath many feet of snow now, making it nearly impossible for us to find anything to eat. We rationed what little food we had very carefully, trying to make it last as long as possible. When our supply of beef was exhausted, we killed our dogs and ate them.

The lack of food made us weak. Some could scarcely walk, and the men had little strength to procure wood. Men, women, and children dragged themselves through the snow from one cabin to another in order to barter for food or other supplies. Little children cried with hunger, and mothers cried because they had so little to give their children.

All too quickly, we were no longer on short allowance, but were simply starving. We had no knowledge about the mountaineers, whether or not they reached Sutter's Fort, and our situation was desperate. My mother then decided that she could wait no longer for help to arrive. Instead, she planned to cross the mountains. She insisted that she would not see her children die without trying to get food for them. She told Patty, Tommy, and James that she would bring them bread, so that they would be willing to stay. Tommy was left with the Breens, Patty with the Kesebergs, and James with the Graves family. Then, with no guide but a compass, my mother, Milt Elliott, our hired girl Eliza, and I started out. Milt wore snowshoes, and we followed in his tracks.

We were in the mountains for five days. Eliza gave out the first day, and she had to return. We kept on, climbing one summit after another, only to see others higher still ahead. Often I would have to crawl up the mountains, being too tired to walk. We had no shelter in which to sleep. Instead, we simply lay on the snow around our fire, listening to the hideous screams of wild beasts somewhere in the distance.

On the third day, we awoke to find ourselves surrounded by a wall of snow. During the night, while in the deep sleep of exhaustion, the heat from our fire had melted the snow around and beneath the blazing logs, and our little camp had gradually sunk many feet below the surface. We had to make our way to the surface very carefully, for any attempt to climb out rapidly might bring an avalanche upon us and bury us alive.

Once we reached the surface, we decided to return to

the lake. My toes had frozen during the night, making walking very painful, and we could not find any of the landmarks that had been described to us, which made it impossible for us to go on. It was fortunate that we decided to return then. Shortly after, a storm came on, the most fearful of the winter, and we would have perished had we not been in our cabin.

We now had nothing to eat but the raw hides on our roof, which we saved when we butchered our cattle. We had to choose between starving or having snow in the cabin. We chose to eat. Our hides, when boiled in water, softened a little, and the water turned into a thick liquid that resembled glue. It was a most unappetizing mixture.

When most of the skins were taken off our roof and we were left without a sound shelter, Patrick Breen kindly gave us a home with his family [January 10]. Mrs. Breen, who still had some beef left, saved my life by slipping me a piece of meat now and then and making sure that I ate it. Even so, my future and that of my family looked bleak indeed, and we were not alone.

# May God Send Help Soon!

*from Patrick Breen's Diary*

January 13—Snowing fast. Snow higher than the shanty. Must be thirteen feet deep. It is dreadful to look at. Don't know how to get wood this morning.

January 15—Mrs. Murphy is blind. Hoping for some account from the mountaineers soon.

January 17—Landrum Murphy crazy last night. Provisions scarce.

January 19—Thawing a little in the sun. Peggy and Edward sick last night. Landrum very low. In great danger if relief doesn't come soon. Hides are all the go [in demand], little else to eat in camp.

January 20—Expecting some person across the mountain this week.

January 21—Denton came this morning with Eliza. She won't eat hides. Mrs. Reed sent her back to live or die on them.

January 26—Cleared up yesterday. Today fine and pleasant. In hopes we are done with snowstorms. Those who went to Sutter's not yet returned. Provisions scant. People getting weak. Living on short allowance of hides.

January 27—Mrs. Keseberg here this morning. Son died three days ago. Mr. Keseberg is sick and Landrum lying in bed the whole of his time. They don't have fire enough to cook their hides. Bill and Simon Murphy sick.

January 30—Fine morning. Beginning to thaw in the sun. More troubles. Mr. and Mrs. Graves seized Mrs. Reed's goods and will hold them until they are paid for goods that Mrs. Reed [used]. Mrs. Reed has no money. Also took most of the hides that Mrs. Reed and family had to live on. May God send help soon.

January 31—Landrum Murphy died last night.

February 3—Mrs. Reed has nothing left but one hide, and it is on the Graves's shanty. Milt is living there and will likely keep that hide. Eddy's child died last night.

February 6—Mrs. Eddy very weak.

February 7—Milt here today. Says Mrs. Reed will get a hide from Mrs. Murphy. McCutchens' child died five days ago.

# Never to Wake Again

## *Virginia Reed Murphy*

Death claimed many in our party by the middle of February. Our handyman, Baylis Williams, who had been in delicate health before we left Springfield, was the first to die at Donner Lake. He passed away before starvation became common in our camp.

The death that affected our family the most was that of Milt Elliott. Mother and I dragged him out of the cabin to bury him. Beginning at his shoes, I patted the pure white snow down softly until I reached the collar on his jacket. Poor Milt! It was hard to cover his face from sight forever, for with his death, our best friend was gone.

I often went to a Catholic church before leaving home, even though my parents did not attend such services. The Breens were the only Catholics in the Donner party, and prayers were said aloud regularly in that cabin every morning and night. While we lived with them, I listened carefully when they prayed.

One fearful night, after we had all gone to bed, I felt that the hour was not far distant when we would go to sleep, never to wake again in this world, like Baylis and Milt. All at once, I found myself on my knees with my hands clasped, looking up through the darkness, making a vow that I would become a Catholic if God would send us relief and let me see my father again.

# Toward Donner Lake

*prepared from notes written by James Reed**

After James Reed left the wagon train in early October, he was joined by Walter Herron, one of Reed's drivers, on his six-hundred mile trek to Sutter's Fort. Their scanty supplies soon gave out. They found a little game along the banks of the Humboldt River, but after leaving the river, they saw none at all. For seven days they journeyed through that wilderness, during which time they ate but two meals, which were made of wild onions. Fortunately, shortly after, they reached the Bear River valley, where they found a small party of emigrants who awaited the arrival of supplies from Johnson's, the first house in the California settlements. Herron, unable to go any further, decided to remain with the emigrants until he regained his strength while Reed, after securing a few supplies, pushed on.

To Reed's great delight, he met Charles Stanton near Johnson's. Stanton did not recognize Reed at first, who

*from "Narrative of the Suffering of a Company of Emigrants in the Mountains of California in the Winter of 1846–47."

*This illustration of a man crossing the mountains gives an idea of what mountain summits were like before winter set in. It's the kind of landscape that James Reed would have found when he crossed the Sierra Nevada the first time. Painting by Thomas Moran of the Hayden survey team, 1871. Courtesy of the Beinecke Rare Book and Manuscript Library, Yale University.*

suffered much from his difficult journey. During the seven days of starvation, Reed had traveled successively thirty-eight, thirty-five, twenty-five, thirty, twenty-six, twenty, and seventeen miles each day, his travels becoming much shorter toward the end as his strength declined.

Stanton, along with William McCutchen, had been sent to Sutter's Fort to get supplies shortly before Reed left the wagon train. Reed was informed that McCutchen, exhausted from the difficult trip, was at the fort resting.

Stanton, however, was on his way back to the Donner party.

Although Captain Sutter had provided Stanton with flour, dried meat, mules, and two of his best Indian guides, Reed did not believe that the supplies were sufficient for the support of the company all the way to Sutter's Fort. After discussing the matter, the men decided that Reed would go to Sacramento to get additional aid. Meanwhile, Stanton would deliver his supplies, then lead the Donner party across the summit to the Bear River valley, where Reed would meet the train with more food.

When Reed reached the fort, he was received at the gate by the generous-hearted Sutter. Sutter furnished him with large quantities of flour and meat, twenty-six horses, and a number of Indians. Here Reed found William Mc-Cutchen. Now somewhat rested from the exhausting journey, McCutchen joined Reed in his attempt to reach the Donner party in the Bear River valley.

They left the fort in late October. Two days after the men began their trek, it rained, and on the third day, the tops of the mountains were covered with snow. When the men reached the Bear River valley, no one from the Donner party was waiting for them.

Reed and McCutchen had no way of knowing that the Donner party was snowbound. Believing that the wagon train had been delayed and expecting to meet it somewhere along the trail, Reed and McCutchen then decided to work their way toward the summit. The next day's march brought them to snow thirty inches in depth.

*Sutter's Fort was really a small city inside a wall. It had its own well, flour mill, blacksmith shop, gunsmith shop, lumber room, bakery, cor-*

Here the Indians deserted them, and on this account, Reed and McCutchen were obliged to leave nine horses in camp.

Starting with seventeen horses, they proceeded to try to cross the mountains. As they advanced, the snow became deeper. When they reached the depth of four feet, the horses were completely exhausted, and it was impossible to proceed with them. Nevertheless, Reed and Mc-Cutchen were still determined to meet their friends and family. Choosing the best horses, they urged them forward—but alas!—the animals couldn't go on.

*rals, administrative offices, jail, and private living quarters. It was forti-
fied with cannon. Courtesy of the Library of Congress.*

The men then attempted to proceed on foot, but for
the want of snowshoes, they were obliged to abandon all
hopes of continuing. They were less than twelve miles
from the summit.

Gathering their horses, they returned to the valley
and went from there to Mr. Johnson's, who received them
in the most hospitable manner. Here they asked for information about crossing the mountains, hoping to find an
easier route. Everyone discouraged them from trying to go
back to their friends at that time. The snow, they said, was
so deep, it would be impossible to reach the camp.

Unwilling to give up, they went to Sutter's Fort, throwing themselves once again upon the generosity of the ever-kind Sutter. Here Reed was also told that it would be impossible for him to attempt to reach his family before February 1, when the worst of the winter storms should cease.

Reed then went to Lower California to seek aid from that quarter. After arriving at the Pueblo de los Angelos, he met Lt. R. F. Pinkney, the American commander in charge of the area. Reed begged for relief, but Pinkney told him that he could do little at the moment. Ever since the Californians had rebelled against Mexican rule, which had begun while the Donner party was on the trail, every American male in the area was busy driving the Mexicans out of California.

Under these circumstances, Reed had but one alternative: to get the help of his countrymen he first had to help them. He then volunteered for a company of mounted riflemen. Fortunately, a decisive battle was fought shortly after upon the Santa Clara plains, and Reed's unit returned to San Francisco, where it disbanded.

Now the citizens turned their attention toward their suffering countrymen in the mountains. A meeting was called in San Francisco, and more than $1,000 was raised. Another $300 was contributed by sailors aboard two ships in the harbor. A committee then purchased supplies and placed them aboard a launch under the command of S. E. Woodworth, who was to take the supplies to the mouth of the Feather River. Meanwhile, Reed was to hire a suf-

*This illustration of Yerba Buena (San Francisco) was based on a photograph taken in 1850. Although the general appearance of the city, the harbor, and the surrounding mountains would have been the same as the first time that James Reed saw the city in 1847, the number of houses increased greatly during the next three years. Courtesy of the Dover Pictorial Archives.*

ficient number of men, purchase horses, and proceed by land to the river. There he would pack his horses with the supplies and go forward to the mountains.

Just as the rescue party was about to leave, a launch belonging to Sutter came in from Sacramento, bringing news of the Donner party. Two men and five women [William Eddy, William Foster, Amanda McCutchen, Mary Graves, Sarah Murphy Foster, Harriet Murphy Pike, and Sarah Graves Fosdick, the only survivors of the fifteen-member snowshoe group, which left the lake on December 16] had arrived at Johnson's.

## Public Meeting

The following announcement appeared on February 6, 1847, in the *California Star*, a newspaper in Yerba Buena, which is now known as San Francisco:

It will be recollected that in a previous [issue] of our paper, we called the attention of our citizens to the situation of a company of unfortunate emigrants now in the California mountains. For the purpose of making their situation more fully known to the people and to adopt measures for their relief, a public meeting was called by the Honorable Washington A. Bartlett, on Wednesday evening last. The citizens generally attended, and in a very short time, the sum of $800 was [raised] to purchase provisions, clothing, horses, and mules to bring in the emigrants. Committees were appointed to call on those who could not attend the meeting, and there is no doubt but that $500 or $600 more will be raised. This speaks well for Yerba Buena.

William Eddy, more dead than alive, had continued on to Sutter's Fort to get help for those starving in the mountains, giving the party's exact location. After Sutter heard Eddy's story about the suffering at Donner Lake and believing that the worst of the storms was behind, he, with the help of two other men, fitted out a relief party, which was now on its way toward the lake.

Upon hearing about the conditions at the winter camp, Reed was certain that more than one group would be needed to save the emigrants in the mountains. Reed and McCutchen then continued with their preparations. They were joined by William Eddy, who quickly proved to be too weak to make the trip, seven hired men, and Hiram Miller, Reed's old friend who had left the Donner wagon train when it took the Hastings Cutoff. Miller had reached California before Reed arrived. When the men had everything they needed, they rushed to the mouth of the Feather River, where they planned to meet the launch loaded with supplies. But to their great disappointment, they found that the boat had not reached the meeting spot.

Believing that no time should be lost, Reed and McCutchen pushed on to Johnson's, where the two men now planned to get supplies. The others were to meet Reed at the ranch shortly after.

Johnson was most generous. He ordered his Indian workers to grind a large quantity of flour, which was to be made into bread. Five beeves were slaughtered, and the men worked all night to preserve the meat by drying it over a fire. The whole process went so well that when Reed's party arrived, little had to be done except to pack the horses. After asking Johnson to tell Woodworth to hasten on with all possible speed when he reached Johnson's ranch, Reed started toward the summit once again.

# Relief!

## *Virginia Reed Murphy*

On the evening of February 19, fourteen days after leaving Sutter's Fort, a rescue party of seven men organized by Sutter, Sinclair, and McKinstry, reached our cabin. The rescuers shouted to attract attention, and Mr. Breen climbed up the icy steps from our nearly buried cabin to the snow's surface to investigate. Shortly after, we heard Mr. Breen shout, "Relief! Thank God! Relief!"

There was joy at Donner Lake that night. But with the joy, sorrow was strangely blended. So many had not survived to share this moment, and they lay all about us, for the living no longer had the strength to bury their dead. And as our story unfolded and our rescuers looked about at the sad scene before them, these strong men sat down and wept.

For several days, members of the relief party distributed food and attempted to pick out the strongest emigrants, those they felt might be able to climb the summit and endure many days of snow and cold without shelter. They eventually chose twenty-three members [Mrs. Reed and her children, Jimmy, Patty, Virginia, and Tommy; George Donner, Jr., and his sisters, Elitha and Leanna; Eliza Williams; Noah James; two of the Breens' children, Edward and Simon; two of the Murphys' children, Mary and William; young Naomi Pike; Mrs. Keseberg and her daughter Ada; William Graves and his sisters, Lovina and Eleanor; Mrs. Wolfinger; John Denton; and young William Hook]. Those left behind were to eat and rest until they were able to leave with other rescuers, who, hopefully, would be able to come and go until all were safely out of the mountains.

On February 22, my family left with the first rescue party. It was a bright, sunny morning, and we were so happy, so hopeful. But we had not gone far when my brother and sister, Tommy and Patty, gave out. They simply didn't have the strength to go on without frequent rests, and one of the leaders, Mr. Glover, thought it was too dangerous to allow them to proceed, for to do so would certainly slow down the party and greatly increase the risk of no one reaching safety before the food gave out. He informed Mama that Tommy and Patty would have to be sent back to the cabins to await the next expedition.

What words can express our feelings? My mother said that she would go back with her children, that we would all go back together. This the relief party would not permit. The men were determined to save every life they could, and they would not risk Mama's life by letting her return, since there was always a chance that the next rescue party might not get through and she might die at the lake. It was better, they said, for her to continue to try to reach the valley. To make the parting easier, Mr. Glover promised Mama that as soon as we reached help in the Bear River valley, he personally would return for her children.

My mother just stood there for a moment, trying to decide what to do. My father was a Mason, and Mama had great faith in the word of a fellow member. Finally she turned to Mr. Glover and said, "Are you a Mason?"

He replied that he was.

"Will you promise me," Mother said, "on the word of a Mason, that if we do not meet their father on the way, you will return and save my children?"

He pledged himself that he would.

It was a sad parting, a fearful struggle. The men turned aside, not being able to hide their tears. Patty said, "I want to see Papa, but I will stay and take good care of Tommy. I do not want you to come back with us." Mr. Glover took the children back to camp, and he left them in the care of Mr. Breen, after making sure that they would receive ample food.

With sorrowful hearts, we traveled on, walking through the snow in single file. The men wearing snowshoes broke the way, and we followed in their tracks. At night we lay down on the snow to sleep, and in the morning we awoke to find our clothing, even our shoestrings, frozen. At break of day, when the snow still had a heavy crust that would support us, we were again on the trail. The sun, which it would seem would have been welcome, only added to our misery now. It softened the snow's crust so much that we broke through with every step and repeatedly sank into the soft snow below, making walking a slow, difficult process, especially in our weak condition. Worse yet, the sun's reflection off the bright white snow nearly blinded us, making it difficult to follow any trail.

My brother, Jimmy, was too small to walk in the tracks made by the men. In order to travel, he had to place one knee on the little hill of snow after each step before swinging his other leg over the mound to reach a footprint. Mother coaxed him along, telling him that with every step he took, he was getting closer to Papa. He was the youngest child [five years old] to walk over the Sierra Nevada Mountains.

On our second day, John Denton gave out. He declared that it would be impossible for him to travel on, but he begged his companions to continue their journey. A fire was built for him, and he was left lying on a bed of freshly cut pine boughs, smoking peacefully. He looked so comfortable that my brother wanted to stay with him. His last thoughts seemed to have gone back to his childhood home, as a little poem about England was found beside his frozen body by the next relief party.

On the way to our cabins, the rescue party had lightened its packs by caching a large quantity of bread and meat, which was to be our main source of food for the trek down the mountain. But when we reached the cache, we were horrified upon learning that animals had destroyed it. Once again, starvation stared us in the face, and we stopped to rest while we waited for our rescuers to find their next cache and return with it.

At the same time, my father was hurrying over the

mountains, and he met us in our hour of need with his hands full of bread! He brought ten men with him. Some members of his party were ahead of him, and when they saw us coming, they called out, "Is Mrs. Reed with you? If she is, tell her Mr. Reed is here."

We heard the call. Mama, overcome with emotion, fell to her knees in the snow while I tried to run to meet Papa. There are no words that can describe the joy we felt when we saw him again.

# Half-eaten Bodies

*prepared from notes written by James Reed**

After an emotional reunion with his wife, son, and daughter, Mr. Reed bid them a tearful farewell. They continued down the mountains, and he pushed on with his party for the cabins. He was in the most dreadful state of anxiety, for members of the first rescue team had informed him that they had found the people at Donner Lake in the worst condition possible.

Before resuming his march, however, Reed sent two of his men back to one of the caches to bring more food forward, believing that he did not have enough supplies to ease the great need he now anticipated. His men were also to leave word that Woodworth was to proceed as fast as he could. Because Reed was emptying one cache, he depended upon Woodworth for future supplies for anyone he would bring out of the mountains.

After two exhausting days, Reed and his men finally saw the top of a cabin just peering above the surface of the

*from "Narrative of the Suffering of a Company of Emigrants in the Mountains of California in the Winter of 1846–47."

snow. As they approached it, Mr. Reed saw his daughter, sitting upon the corner of the roof, her feet resting upon the snow. Little could exceed the joy of each when they saw each other. A few mintues later, Reed entered the cabin where he found his son Tommy—alive!

Members of the rescue party immediately began to distribute food, and as they worked their way from one cabin to another, they saw much that horrified them. Between the cabins lay fleshless bones and half-eaten bodies of those who had starved to death, corpses whose flesh had been eaten by those struggling to stay alive. In one of the cabins, the men found children devouring the heart and liver of their father, and in another, they found a skull in a camp kettle, truly shocking sights!

Yet while gazing upon these gruesome items, Reed was reminded of the party's desire to live, and he thought about the cruel fate that had overtaken his companions and cut them down, almost in sight of a beautiful country where they could have lived in peace and plenty. Horrid as the reminders were, he could not condemn the survivors.

Instead, Reed continued to distribute supplies and study the living, trying to decide who was able to travel. He was ready to lead as many people as possible to safety at Sutter's Fort.

# A Terrible Foreboding

*from James Reed's Journal*

March 1—Gave food to Keseberg, Breen, and Graves. Then two of my party left for the Donners' camp, five miles away. Informed the people who were able to travel that we start day after tomorrow. Made soup for the infirm, washed and clothed afresh Mrs. Eddy and Fosters' children, and rendered every assistance in our power. I left Mr. Stone with the Kesebergs. He is to cook and watch the eating of Mrs. Murphy, Keseberg, and three children.

March 2—Left early this morning with three of my men and went to the Donners. Only three children of Jacob Donner can come with us. Three more children at George Donner's can travel. His wife is also able but prefers to stay with her husband, who is very ill, until provisions from Woodworth arrive, which are confidently expected. Left two of my men in this camp to help the infirm. Got back to the cabins about eight o'clock, much worn down. Men here helped Mrs. Graves cache about $800 worth of gold and silver, too heavy to carry.

March 3—Left with the following persons: Mr. and Mrs.

Patrick Breen and their children, John [14], Patrick [11], Peter [7], James [4], and Isabella [1], two of whom had to be carried; Solomon Hook [14]; Mary [7] and Isaac Donner [5]; Mrs. Graves and four of her children, Jonathan [7], Nancy [9], Franklin, Jr. [5], and Elizabeth [1], two to be carried; and two children of my own, Patty [8] and Tommy [3], in all seventeen souls. Proceeded about two miles and camped on the edge of the lake.

March 4—Left camp early. Traveled on the lake and camped under the mountain. Made about four miles today.

March 5—After breakfast, I had two scanty meals left for all. I sent ahead three of my best men, one to bring up the first cache, the others the second. After a fatiguing day, arrived at a spot called Starved Camp at the head of the Juba River. Here my men began to fail, being for several days on half allowance or one and a half pints of gruel [a thin, cooked cereal, such as oatmeal] per day. The sky looks like snow, and everything indicates a storm. God forbid. Wood being got for the night and boughs for the beds of all. Night closing fast and the clouds thickening. Terror! Terror! I feel a terrible foreboding, but I dare not communicate my feelings to anyone. Death to all if our provisions do not come in a day or two and a storm should fall on us. Very cold.

March 6/7—Still in camp. The last of our provisions gone. Waiting anxiously for supplies. None come.

My dreaded storm is now upon us. Snowing began in the first part of the night and with the snow came howling winds. A great crying among the children and praying and lamentations among the parents on account of the cold and dread of death from the storm. My men up nearly all night making fires. Some of the men began to pray. It has snowed twelve inches, still the storm continues. The snow blows so thick that we cannot see twenty feet, looking against the wind. I dread the coming night. Only three are able to get wood.

After some time, wood being secured, we had a great difficulty in fixing a foundation for our fire to keep the fire from melting the snow beneath and disappearing into a well, now fifteen feet deep and no earth in sight.

Still storming. Very cold. So cold that the few men employed in cutting the [dead] trees have to come and warm themselves about every ten minutes. Hunger, hunger is the cry from the children and nothing to give them. Freezing is the cry of the mothers. Night closing fast and with it the winds increase. Not quite so much snow falling as before.

March 8—Thank God! Day has once more appeared, although darkened by the storm. The hurricane of winds never ceased for even ten minutes at a time during one of the most dismal nights I ever witnessed, and I hope I never shall witness such again. Several times I expected to see the people perish from the extreme cold. At one time our fire was nearly gone, and had it not been for McCutchen's exertions, it would have entirely disappeared. If the fire had been lost, two thirds of the people would have been out of their misery before morning. I am exhausted.

# A World So Beautiful

## Virginia Reed Murphy

On the third night of the furious snowstorm, my father became so weak that he could no longer help anyone, and he would have died but for the exertions of William Mc-Cutchen and Hiram Miller, who worked over him all night. From this time forward, the toil and responsibility of this rescue team rested upon these two men.

When the storm at last ceased, McCutchen and Miller were determined to set out over the snow with those who could travel and send back relief to those not able to walk. Miller picked up Tommy and started. Patty thought she could walk, but gradually everything faded from her sight, and she, too, seemed to be dying. My father found some bread crumbs in his mitten, and after she ate these, she seemed somewhat revived. Papa then picked up Patty and carried her, and the heat from his body helped keep her alive.

# Roster of Dead
*(approximate ages given in parentheses)*

*James Reed group (eleven members):*
James Smith (24), late November, in winter camp
at Alder Creek
Baylis Williams (24), December 16, in winter camp
Milt Elliott (28), February 9, in winter camp
*George and Jacob Donner group (twenty-three members):*
Luke Halloran (25), August 29, on the trail
Jacob Donner (65), late November, in winter camp
Samuel Shoemaker (25), late November, in winter camp
Charles Stanton (35), December 21, with snowshoers
Antonio (23), December 24, with snowshoers
John Denton (28), February 24, with Sutter's rescue team
William Hook (12), February 28, with Sutter's rescue team
Elizabeth Donner (45), March, in winter camp
Isaac Donner (5), March 7, with Reed's rescue team
Lewis Donner (3), March 7 or 8, in winter camp
Samuel Donner (4), April 1, in winter camp
George Donner (62), April, in winter camp
Tamsen Donner (45), April, in winter camp
*Breen-Dolan group (ten members):*
Patrick Dolan (40), December 25, with snowshoers
*Eddy group (four members):*
Margaret Eddy (1), February 2, in winter camp
Eleanor Eddy (25), February 7, in winter camp
James Eddy (3), March, in winter camp
*Keseberg group (six members):*
Mr. Hardcoop (60 + ), about October 8, abandoned on trail
Karl Burger (30), December 29, in winter camp
Louis Keseberg, Jr. (1), January 24, in winter camp

Ada Keseberg (3), about February 25, with
Sutter's rescue team
*Wolfinger group (two members):*
Mr. Wolfinger (30?), October 13, on the trail; murdered by
Spitzer and Reinhardt
*Spitzer and Reinhardt group (two members):*
Joseph Reinhardt (30), late November, in winter camp
Augustus Spitzer (30), February 7, in winter camp
*McCutchen group (three members):*
Harriet (1), February 2, in winter camp
*Murphy–Foster–Pike group (thirteen members):*
William Pike (25), October 20, accidental shooting on trail
Lemuel Murphy (12), December 27, with snowshoers
Landrum Murphy (15), January 31, in winter camp
Catherine Pike (1), February 20, in winter camp
George Foster (4), early March, in winter camp
Lavina Murphy (50), March 19, in winter camp
*Graves–Fosdick group (thirteen members):*
John Snyder (25), October 5, killed by James Reed on trail
Franklin Graves, Sr. (57), December 24, with snowshoers
Jay Fosdick (23), January 5, with snowshoers
Elizabeth Graves (47), March 8, with Reed's rescue team
Franklin Graves, Jr. (5), March 8, with Reed's rescue team
Elizabeth Graves, Jr. (1), died shortly after arriving at
Sutter's Fort with Reed's rescue team
*Two Indians sent with Stanton to help the Donner party:*
Luis, January, with snowshoers; killed by William Foster
Salvador, January, with snowshoers; killed by Foster

When this rescue team stumbled into Woodworth's camp, who had so far refused to send men into a storm in the mountains, a third relief party started for the lake both to help those left along the trail and to bring out as many others as possible. This time Simon Murphy; Frances, Georgia, and Eliza Donner; and John Baptiste Trubode were brought out.

In mid-April, a fourth relief went to the lake. By this time, only Louis Keseberg was alive. Shortly after, he joined the other survivors at the fort. Out of the eighty-three persons who were snowed in at Donner Lake, forty-two perished, and out of the thirty-one emigrants who left Springfield, Illinois, that bright spring morning, only eighteen lived to reach California.

Captain Sutter did all he could to help the sufferers, as did several others in the area. Mr. Sinclair, one of the men who helped organize the first rescue party, took Mama, Jimmy, and me to his home. Mrs. Sinclair was the dearest of women, and we were surrounded with every comfort. I will never forget their kindness.

But when we first arrived, our anxiety was not over. We knew that my father's party had been caught in the storm. I can still see my mother, leaning against the door for hours at a time, looking toward the mountains.

But at last my father arrived at Mr. Sinclair's with the little ones, and our family was united. That day's great happiness repaid us for much that we had suffered.

It was spring now, and words cannot tell how beautiful that season or the area appeared to those of us coming out of the mountains from our little dark cabins under the snow. Before us lay the broad valley of the Sacramento River, and we rejoiced in its great beauty.

One day, shortly after we arrived, while traveling down the Napa valley, we stopped at noon to have lunch under the shade of an oak. I was not hungry; I was too full of the beauty around me to think of eating, so I wandered off by myself to a lovely little knoll. I simply stood there in a bed of wildflowers, looking up and down the green valley. The birds were singing in the branches over my head, and the sun was smiling down upon all. I drank it all in for a moment, kissed my hand, then gently blew the kisses from my palm toward heaven in thanksgiving to the Almighty for creating a world so beautiful.

# Afterword

Newspapers in the San Francisco area carried stories about the Donner party for years. The first articles appeared in late 1846 when editors learned that a party of emigrants was snowbound in the Sierras. Shortly after, reporters covered fund-raising events in San Francisco when James Reed was trying to organize a relief party, and later, as members of the wagon train were brought out, these same reporters interviewed the survivors. In addition, whenever someone from the party died in the years to come, the fact that he or she was a member of the Donner party was usually mentioned in the obituary.

At first, there was a general feeling of relief among readers when it was announced that at least some of the snowbound emigrants had managed to make it out of the mountains. Readers were eager to know all about the survivors and the heroic efforts of the rescue parties. But when stories about cannibalism began to circulate, the public's attention quickly turned to the gory details, and people ignored the rest of the story about the Donner party's life-and-death struggle.

The sensational accounts were further fueled by accusations of murder. Snowshoer William Foster was accused of killing Luis and Salvador, the two Indians whom

Sutter had sent with Stanton to help the emigrants. Accusers said that Foster found the nearly dead men along the trail shortly after they left the snowshoers and that he killed the Indians so that he could eat them. Then Louis Keseberg was accused of killing Tamsen Donner at the winter camp so that he could eat her. Keseberg, who insisted that Donner had died from starvation, did little to help his position when he repeatedly horrified and disgusted listeners by describing how good Tamsen tasted.

While many people were greatly upset by the acts of cannibalism, most were not willing to condemn the survivors if the victim had died from natural causes. This was especially true when the survivors were parents who were struggling to stay alive so that they could try to save their children. Few people, though, could accept killing someone for his or her flesh. Even so, no one in the train was ever formally charged with murder. Instead, the accusations hung over the heads of the suspected murderers. In Keseberg's case, the accusation haunted him until he died in 1895. After Keseberg's death, the accusations were included in books and articles about the Donner party, more than fifty of which have been published to date.

The search for someone or something to blame for the disaster also kept the story alive. The public lambasted Lansford Hastings and Jim Bridger. People considered the advice that these men had given to the Donner party irresponsible at best. Others found fault with the leaders of the wagon train. In the eyes of these people, the train's leaders were overconfident, almost cocky. The critics pointed out that the leaders refused to listen to warnings

*The Reeds' home in San Jose. Mr. Reed is pictured on the far left with Tommy and Patty. Courtesy of the California State Department of Parks, Sutter's Fort State Historic Park.*

about the dangers of the cutoff from other emigrants and that they traveled too slowly, held back by big wagons—especially the Reeds' palace car—and too many belongings. The party's leisurely pace, the critics added, greatly increased its risk of getting snowbound, especially when the first storms—another source of blame—arrived earlier in the season than usual.

The attention given to the survivors and their story made it difficult for the emigrants to put their ordeal behind them. Still the cockiness that had gotten them into trouble on the trail and the confidence that enabled them to overcome disaster helped them to build new lives.

Virginia's family found success and happiness in Cal-

*Mrs. Virginia Reed Murphy. Courtesy of Bancroft Library, The University of California, Berkeley.*

ifornia. When gold was discovered on Captain Sutter's land and in the surrounding mines in 1848, nearly everyone in the area, including James Reed, became a prospector. Reed found gold, and he used his wealth to buy land and to build a home in San Jose. Mr. and Mrs. Reed lived there for many years along with their four children and adopted daughter, Mary Donner, who was orphaned at Donner Lake. Mrs. Reed died on November 25, 1861, and her husband passed away on July 24, 1874. They were buried in San Jose, and according to legend, their coffins touch.

Virginia, who kept her promise to become a Catholic, married John M. Murphy (no relation to the Murphys in the wagon train), when she was fifteen years old. Murphy had discovered gold, and he was a wealthy man. He was also involved in politics in San Jose, and he held public office there. The Murphys had nine children, three of whom died while they were infants. Virginia died in 1931 at the age of ninety-eight.

California's beauty continually amazed Virginia, and she often encouraged others to join her in San Jose, so that they too, might see the area's lush green valleys and snow-capped mountains. She wrote letters to friends in Illinois, telling them all about the area's great beauty, and to make the trip easier for them than hers had been, she ended her letters with a little advice. "Bring nothing but provisions and just enough clothing to last until you get here," she wrote, "and don't take any cutoffs."

# Bibliography

Burns, Ric. "On the Oregon Trail." *American Heritage,* (May/June, 1993): 60–66.

Hill, William E. *The Oregon Trail: Yesterday and Today.* Caldwell, Idaho: Caxton Printers, 1987.

Lewis, Oscar. *Sutter's Fort: Gateway to the Gold Fields.* Englewood Cliffs, N. J.: Prentice-Hall, 1966.

McGlashan, Charles Fayette. *History of the Donner Party: A Tragedy of the Sierras.* Truckee, Calif.: Crowley & McGlashan, 1879.

Merryman, J. H. "Narrative of the Suffering of a Company of Emigrants in the Mountains of California in the Winter of 1846–47." *Illinois Journal* (December 9, 1847): l.

Murphy, Virginia Reed. "Across the Plains in the Donner Party: A Personal Narrative of the Overland Trip to California 1846–47." *Century Magazine* (Vol. XLII, 1891).

Pigney, Joseph. *For Fear We Shall Perish: The Story of the Donner Party Disaster.* New York: E. P. Dutton, 1961.

Reed, James. Letters. *Sangamo Journal,* (July 30 and November 5, 1846): l.

Reed, Virginia. Letter. *Illinois Journal,* (December 16, 1847): l.

Stewart, George, R. *Ordeal by Hunger: The Story of the Donner Party.* Boston: Houghton Mifflin, 1960.
Wukovits, John F. "Dire Warning Ignored." *Wild West* (April 1, 1992): 34–41.

# For More Information

Several famous people mentioned in *Across the Plains in the Donner Party* are subjects of other books. For more information about Captain Sutter, read Glenn Clairmonte's book, *John Sutter of California* (New York: Nelson, 1954). For more information about artist William H. Jackson, see Beaumont Newhall and Diana E. Edkin's book, *William H. Jackson* (Fort Worth, Tex.: Amon Carter Museum, 1974). This book of photos contains many of Jackson's earliest pictures of the West. A chronology in the back of the book includes entries from his diaries, which he wrote while he traveled across the plains and over the mountains.

George Sanderlin's book, *The Settlement of California* (New York: Coward, McCann & Geoghegen, 1972) devotes several chapters to life in California in the 1800s. He explains what California was like when the first emigrants arrived, and he discusses the Gold Rush, which began on Captain Sutter's property.

For more information about the West, check out *Westward on the Oregon Trail* (New York: American Heritage Publishing, 1962, Junior Library), Leonard Everett Fisher's *The Oregon Trail* (New York: Holiday House, 1990), and *The Great American West: A Pictorial History from Coronado to the Last Frontier* by James D. Horan (New York: Crown Publishers, 1959). Horan's book, meant for good readers, has many pictures worth studying and a whole chapter on buffalo.

And finally, for more information about wagons, see *Conestogas and Stagecoaches* by Tim McNeese (New York: Crestwood, 1993).